REAL LEADERSHIP

THE 101 COLLECTION

John C. Maxwell

NELSON BUSINESS
A Division of Thomas Nelson Publishers
Since 1798

www.thomasnelson.com

Nelson Business books may be purchased in bulk for educational, business, fundraising, or sales promotional use. For information, please email SpecialMarkets@ThomasNelson.com.

ISBN 0-7852-8844-9

Printed in the United States of America

06 07 08 09 10 QW 5 4 3 2 1

RELATIONSHIPS

101

WHAT EVERY LEADER NEEDS TO KNOW

JOHN C. MAXWELL

NELSON BUSINESS
A Division of Thomas Nelson Publishers
Since 1798

www.thomasnelson.com

Published in Nashville, Tennessee, by Thomas Nelson, Inc.

Portions of this book were previously published in *Becoming a Person of Influence, The 17 Essential Qualities of a Team Player, The 21 Irrefutable Laws of Leadership, The 21 Indispensable Qualities of a Leader,* and *Your Road Map for Success.*

Library of Congress Cataloging-in-Publication Data

Maxwell, John C., 1947–
Relationships 101 : what every leader needs to know / John C. Maxwell.
p. cm.
"Portions of this book were previously published in *Becoming a person of influence, The 17 essential qualities of a team player, The 21 irrefutable laws of leadership, The 21 indispensable qualities of a leader,* and *Your road map for success."*
ISBN 0-7852-6351-9 (hardcover)
1. Leadership. 2. Interpersonal relations. 3. Success in business.
I. Title.
HD57.7 .M39427
658.4'092—dc22
2003021381

CONTENTS

PUBLISHER'S PREFACE

No one undertakes a journey alone. We depend upon others constantly—in ways both tangible and intangible—to move us toward our destination. We cannot succeed without the help of others, but forming positive relationships can be a challenge. In *Relationships 101,* John Maxwell reveals the secrets behind connecting with other people. He points out the barriers to relationships, emphasizes the shared needs among people, and describes the ways to connect with others on many different levels. Naturally, he also shows how relationships impact leadership. Most of all, he explains how relationships help us reach our fullest potential.

As America's leadership expert, Dr. Maxwell has spent a lifetime helping others become successful. Through this series of books, his goal is to help others become a REAL success in four crucial areas: Relationships, Equipping, Attitude, and Leadership. *Relationships 101* provides the fundamentals you need to master relationship skills. *Equipping 101, Attitude*

101, and *Leadership 101* will give you the other skills you need to reach your goals.

We are delighted to publish *Relationships 101* because we recognize the significance of positive relationships in every aspect of life. Building positive relationships with others involves risk, but Dr. Maxwell shows that the rewards outweigh that risk. This short course on relationships will equip you with valuable skills for connecting with others as you journey toward success.

PART I

THE NATURE
OF RELATIONSHIPS

I

WHY ARE RELATIONSHIPS IMPORTANT TO SUCCESS?

Relationships are the glue that holds team members together.

In the early 1960s, Michael Deaver was a young man with a political bent looking for a leader he could believe in and follow. The person he found was an actor-turned-politician named Ronald Reagan. In 1966, Reagan was elected governor of California, an office he would hold for two terms, from 1967 to 1975. During that tenure, Deaver became Reagan's deputy chief of staff, an office he also held when Reagan became the nation's fortieth president.

Deaver admired many things about the man he worked with for thirty years: his convictions and love of country, his understanding of himself, his skill as a communicator, and his honesty. Deaver said, "I would go so far as to say that he was actually incapable of dishonesty."[1] But perhaps what was most impressive about Ronald Reagan was his ability to relate to people.

Deaver commented, "Ronald Reagan was one of the shyest

men I'd ever met."[2] Yet the president was able to connect with anyone, whether a head of state, a blue-collar worker, or a feisty member of the press. When asked about why Reagan had such rapport with the press corps, Deaver remarked, "Well, Reagan basically liked people, whether they were part of the press corps or whether they were just ordinary people. That comes through. While many of the press wouldn't agree with Reagan's policy, they genuinely liked him as a person."[3]

Part of Reagan's skill came from his natural charisma and glib verbal aptitude developed in Hollywood. But even greater was his ability to relate to people, something he honed while traveling the country for a decade as the spokesman for General Electric.

It's said that Reagan could make anyone feel like his best friend, even someone he'd never met before. But more important, he connected with the people closest to him. He truly cared about the people on his team. "The chief of staff, or the gardener, or a secretary would all be treated the same, as far as he was concerned," remembered Deaver. "They were all important."[4]

Deaver related a story that tells much about the connection the two men experienced. In 1975, Reagan gave a speech to a group of conservation-minded hunters in San Francisco, and the organization gave him a small bronze lion as a gift. At the time, Deaver admired it and told Governor Reagan how beautiful he thought it was.

Ten years later, Deaver prepared to bring his service to President Reagan to an end after having written his letter of resignation. Reagan asked Deaver to come to the Oval Office the next morning. As the deputy chief of staff entered the room, the president stood in front of his desk to greet him.

"Mike," he said, "all night I've been trying to think of something to give you that would be a reminder of all the great times we had together." Then Reagan turned around and picked up something from his desk. "You kinda liked this little thing, as I recall," the president said, his eyes moist. And he handed the bronze lion to Deaver, who was totally overcome. He couldn't believe that Reagan had remembered that about him all those years. That lion has held a place of honor in Deaver's home ever since.

SOLID RELATIONSHIPS

Everyone liked being around Ronald Reagan because he loved people and connected with them. He understood that relationships were the glue that held his team members together—the more solid the relationships, the more cohesive his team.

Just about everything you do depends on teamwork. It

doesn't matter whether you are a leader or follower, coach or player, teacher or student, parent or child, CEO or nonprofit worker; you will be involved with other people. The question is, will your involvement with others be successful? Your best chance for leadership also depends upon connecting with those on your team. Here is how you know whether you have built solid relationships with others. Look for the following five characteristics in your relationships:

1. RESPECT

When it comes to relationships, everything begins with respect, with the desire to place value on other people. Human relations author Les Giblin said, "You can't make the other fellow feel important in your presence if you secretly feel that he is a nobody."

The thing about respect is that you should show it to others, even before they have done anything to warrant it, simply because they are human beings. But at the same time, you should always expect to have to earn it from others. And the place you earn it the quickest is on difficult ground.

2. SHARED EXPERIENCES

Respect can lay the foundation for a good relationship, but it alone is not enough. You can't be relational with someone you don't know. It requires shared experiences over time. And that's not always easy to achieve. For example, right after Brian Billick, coach of the Baltimore Ravens, won the 2001 Super Bowl, he was asked about the team's chances for repeating a championship season. He commented that it would be very difficult. Why? Because 25 to 30 percent of the team changes every year. Newer players don't have the shared experiences with the team that are needed to succeed.

3. TRUST

When you respect people and you spend enough time with them to develop shared experiences, you are in a position to develop trust. Trust is essential to all good relationships. Scottish poet George MacDonald observed, "To be trusted is a greater compliment than to be loved." Without trust, you cannot sustain any kind of relationship.

4. RECIPROCITY

One-sided personal relationships don't last. If one person is always the giver and the other is always the receiver, then the relationship will eventually disintegrate. The same is true of all relationships, including those on a team. For people to improve relationally, there has to be give-and-take so that everyone benefits as well as gives. Remember to ask your teammates, colleagues, and friends questions about their hopes, desires, and goals. Give people your full attention. Show others you care about them.

> WHEN IT COMES TO RELATIONSHIPS, EVERYTHING
> BEGINS WITH RESPECT, WITH THE DESIRE TO PLACE
> VALUE ON OTHER PEOPLE.

---

5. MUTUAL ENJOYMENT

When relationships grow and start to get solid, the people involved begin to enjoy each other. Just being together can turn even unpleasant tasks into positive experiences.

How are you doing when it comes to being relational? Do you spend a lot of time and energy building solid relationships, or are you so focused on results that you tend to overlook (or overrun) others? If the latter is true of you, think about the wise words of George Kienzle and Edward Dare in *Climbing the Executive Ladder:* "Few things will pay you bigger dividends than the time and trouble you take to understand people. Almost nothing will add more to your stature as an executive and a person. Nothing will give you greater satisfaction or bring you more happiness." Becoming a highly relational person brings individual and team success.

WHAT DO I NEED TO KNOW ABOUT OTHERS?

People don't care how much you know,
until they know how much you care.

If your desire is to be successful and to make a positive impact on your world, you need the ability to understand others. Understanding others gives you the potential to influence every area of life, not just the business arena. For example, look at how understanding people helped this mother of a preschooler. She said:

Leaving my four-year-old son in the house, I ran out to throw something in the trash. When I tried to open the door to get back inside, it was locked. I knew that insisting that my son open the door would have resulted in an hour-long battle of the wills. So in a sad voice, I said, "Oh, too bad. You just locked yourself in the house." The door opened at once.

Understanding people certainly impacts your ability to communicate with others. David Burns, a medical doctor and professor of psychiatry at the University of Pennsylvania, observed, "The biggest mistake you can make in trying to talk convincingly is to put your highest priority on expressing your ideas and feelings. What most people really want is to be listened to, respected, and understood. The moment people see that they are being understood, they become more motivated to understand your point of view." If you can learn to understand people—how they think, what they feel, what inspires them, how they're likely to act and react in a given situation—then you can motivate and influence them in a positive way.

WHY PEOPLE FAIL TO UNDERSTAND OTHERS

Lack of understanding concerning others is a recurrent source of tension in our society. I once heard an attorney say, "Half of all the controversies and conflicts that arise among people are caused not by differences of opinion or an inability to agree, but by the lack of understanding of one another." If we could reduce the number of misunderstandings, the courts wouldn't be as crowded, there would be fewer violent crimes, the divorce rate would go down, and the amount of everyday stress most people experience would drop dramatically.

If understanding is such an asset, why don't more people practice it? There are many reasons:

FEAR

Seventeenth-century American colonist William Penn advised, "Neither despise or oppose what thou dost not understand," yet many people seem to do exactly the opposite. When they don't understand others, they often react by becoming fearful. And once they start fearing others, they rarely try to overcome their fear in order to learn more about them. It becomes a vicious cycle.

Unfortunately, fear is evident in the workplace when it comes to employees' reactions toward their leaders. Yet in a healthy work environment, if you give others the benefit of the doubt and replace fear with understanding, everyone can work together positively. All people have to do is follow the advice of President Harry Truman, who said, "When we understand the other fellow's viewpoint—understand what he is trying to do—nine times out of ten he is trying to do right."

SELF-CENTEREDNESS

When fear isn't a stumbling block, self-centeredness often is. People are not self-centered on purpose; it's just in the nature of humans to think of their own interests first. If you want to see an example of that, play with a two-year-old child. He naturally chooses the best toys for himself and insists on his own way.

One way to overcome our natural self-centeredness is to try to see things from other people's perspectives. Talking to a group of salespeople, Art Mortell, author of *World Class Selling*, shared this experience: "Whenever I'm losing at chess, I consistently get up and stand behind my opponent and see the board from his side. Then I discover the stupid moves I've made because I can see it from his viewpoint. The salesperson's challenge is to see the world from the prospect's viewpoint."[1]

That's the challenge for every one of us, no matter what our profession. The following quote reminds us of what our priorities should be when dealing with other people:

A SHORT COURSE IN HUMAN RELATIONS

The least important word: I

The most important word: We

The two most important words: Thank you.

The three most important words: All is forgiven.

The four most important words: What is your opinion?

The five most important words: You did a good job.

The six most important words: I want to understand you better.

FAILURE TO APPRECIATE DIFFERENCES

The next logical step after leaving behind self-centeredness is learning to recognize and respect everyone else's unique qualities. Instead of trying to cast others in your image, learn to appreciate their differences. If someone has a talent that you don't have, great. The two of you can strengthen each other's weaknesses. If others come from a different culture, broaden your horizons and learn what you can from them. Your new knowledge will help you relate not only to them, but also to others.

Once you learn to appreciate other people's differences, you come to realize that there are many responses to leadership and motivation. Joseph Beck, onetime president of the Kenley Corporation, recognized that truth when he said that "different people are motivated in different ways. A good basketball coach, for example, knows when a player needs a 'kick in the pants.' The main difference is that all players need encouragement and only some need a 'kick in the pants.'"

FAILURE TO ACKNOWLEDGE SIMILARITIES

We all have emotional reactions to what's happening around us. To foster understanding, think of what your emotions would be if you were in the same position as the person you're interacting with. You know what you would want to happen in a given situation. Chances are that the person you're working with has many of the same feelings.

IF YOU TREAT EVERY PERSON YOU MEET AS IF HE OR SHE
WERE THE MOST IMPORTANT PERSON IN THE WORLD, YOU'LL
COMMUNICATE THAT HE OR SHE *IS* SOMEBODY—TO YOU.

THINGS EVERYBODY NEEDS TO UNDERSTAND ABOUT PEOPLE

Knowing what people need and want is the key to understanding them. And if you can understand them, you can influence them and impact their lives in a positive way. What I know about understanding people can be summed up in the following list:

1. EVERYBODY WANTS TO BE SOMEBODY

There isn't a person in the world who doesn't have the desire to be someone, to have significance. Even the least ambitious and unassuming person wants to be regarded highly by others.

I remember the first time these feelings were stirred strongly within me. It was back when I was in the fourth grade and went to my first basketball game. I stood with my buddies in the balcony of the gym. The thing that I remember most wasn't the game; it was the announcement of the starting lineups. They turned all the lights out, and then some spotlights came on. The announcer called out the names of the starters, and they ran out to the middle of the floor one by one with everybody in the place cheering.

I hung over the balcony that day as a fourth-grade kid and said, "Wow, I'd like that to happen to me." In fact, by the time the introductions were over, I looked at my friend Bobby Wilson, and I said, "Bobby, when I get to high school, they're going to announce my name, and I'm going to run out in the spotlight to the middle of that basketball floor. And the people are going to cheer for me because I'm going to be somebody."

I went home that night and told my dad, "I want to be a basketball player." Soon afterward, he got me a Spalding basketball, and we put a goal on the garage. I used to shovel snow off that driveway to practice my foul shots and play basketball because I had a dream of becoming somebody.

It's funny how that kind of dream can impact your life. In the sixth grade, I played intramural basketball. Our team won a couple of games, so we got to go to the Old Mill Street Gym in Circleville, Ohio, where I'd seen that basketball game in the fourth grade. When we got there, instead of going out onto the floor with the rest of the players as they were warming up, I went to the bench where those high school players had been two years before. I sat right where they had, and I closed my eyes (the equivalent of turning the lights out in the gym). Then in my head I heard my name announced, and I ran out in the middle of the floor.

It felt so good to hear the imaginary applause that I thought, *I'll do it again!* So I did. In fact, I did it three times, and all of a sudden, I realized that my buddies weren't playing basketball; they were just watching me in disbelief. But I didn't care because I was one step closer to being the person I'd dreamed about becoming.

Everybody wants to be regarded and valued by others. In other words, everybody wants to be somebody. Once that piece of information becomes a part of your everyday thinking, you'll gain incredible insight into why people do the things they do. And if you treat every person you meet as if he or she were the most important person in the world, you'll communicate that he or she *is* somebody—to you.

2. NOBODY CARES HOW MUCH YOU KNOW UNTIL HE KNOWS HOW MUCH YOU CARE

The moment that people know that you care about them, the way they feel about you changes. Showing others that you care isn't always easy. Your greatest times and fondest memories will come because of people, but so will your most difficult, hurting, and tragic times. People are your greatest assets and your greatest liabilities. The challenge is to keep caring about them no matter what.

I came across an insightful quote called "Paradoxical Commandments of Leadership." Here's what it says:

People are illogical, unreasonable, and self-centered—love them anyway.

If you do good, people will accuse you of selfish ulterior motives—do good anyway.

If you're successful, you'll win false friends and true enemies—succeed anyway.

The good you do today will perhaps be forgotten tomorrow—do good anyway.

Honesty and frankness make you vulnerable—be honest and frank anyway.

The biggest man with the biggest ideas can be shot down by the smallest man with the smallest mind—think big anyway.

People favor underdogs but follow only hot dogs—fight for a few underdogs anyway.

What you spend years building may be destroyed overnight—build anyway.

People really need help but may attack you if you help them—help them anyway.

Give the world the best that you have and you will get

kicked in the teeth—give the world the best that you have anyway.

If better is possible, then good is not enough.

That's the right way to treat people. Besides, you never know which people in your sphere of influence are going to rise up and make a difference in your life and the lives of others.

3. EVERYBODY NEEDS SOMEBODY

Contrary to popular belief, there are no such things as self-made men and women. Everybody needs friendship, encouragement, and help. What people can accomplish by themselves is almost nothing compared to their potential when working with others. And doing things with other people tends to bring contentment. Besides, Lone Rangers are rarely happy people. King Solomon of ancient Israel stated the value of working together this way:

Two are better than one,
    because they have a good return for their work:
If one falls down,
    his friend can help him up.
But pity the man who falls
    and has no one to help him up!

Also, if two lie down together, they will keep warm.
But how can one keep warm alone?
Though one may be overpowered,
two can defend themselves.
A cord of three strands is not quickly broken.[2]

Everybody needs somebody to come alongside and help. If you understand that, are willing to give to others and help them, and maintain the right motives, their lives and yours can change.

4. EVERYBODY CAN BE SOMEBODY WHEN SOMEBODY UNDERSTANDS AND BELIEVES HER

Once you understand people and believe in them, they really can become somebody. And it doesn't take much effort to help other people feel important. Little things, done deliberately at the right time, can make a big difference.

When was the last time you went out of your way to make people feel special, as if they were somebody? The investment required on your part is totally overshadowed by the impact it makes on them. Everyone you know and all the people you meet have the potential to be someone important in the lives of others. All they need is encouragement and motivation from you to help them reach their potential.

5. ANYBODY WHO HELPS SOMEBODY INFLUENCES A LOT OF BODIES

The final thing you need to understand about people is that when you help one person, you're really impacting a lot of other people. What you give to one person overflows into the lives of all the people that person impacts. The nature of influence is to multiply. It even impacts you because when you help others and your motives are good, you always receive more than you can ever give. Most people are so genuinely grateful when another person makes them feel special that they never tire of showing their gratitude.

CHOOSE TO UNDERSTAND OTHERS

In the end, the ability to understand people is a choice. It's true that some people are born with great instincts that enable them to understand how others think and feel. But even if you aren't instinctively a people person, you can improve your ability to work with others. Every person is capable of having the ability to understand, motivate, and ultimately influence others.

PART II

THE BUILDING BLOCKS OF RELATIONSHIPS

3

How Can I Encourage Others?

Believing in people before *they have proved themselves is the key to motivating people to reach their potential.*

Everyone loves encouragement. It lifts them up when they're down and motivates them when they're feeling discouraged. To be an encourager, you need to believe the best in people, to have faith in them. In fact, faith is essential for building and maintaining all positive relationships, yet it's a scarce commodity today. Take a look at the following four facts about faith:

1. Most People Don't Have Faith in Themselves

Not long ago I saw a *Shoe* comic strip by Jeff MacNelly that showed Shoe, the crusty newspaper editor, standing on the mound in a baseball game. His catcher says to him, "You've got to have faith in your curve ball." In the next frame Shoe remarks, "It's easy for him to say. When it comes to believing in myself, I'm an agnostic."

That's the way too many people feel today. They have

trouble believing in themselves. They believe they will fail. Even when they see a light at the end of the tunnel, they're convinced it's a train. They see a difficulty in every responsibility. But the reality is that difficulties seldom defeat people; lack of faith in themselves usually does it. With a little faith in themselves, people can do miraculous things. But without, they have a really tough time.

2. MOST PEOPLE DON'T HAVE SOMEONE WHO HAS FAITH IN THEM

In *Just for Today*, James Keller tells this story: "A sidewalk flower vendor was not doing any business. Suddenly a happy thought struck him and he put up this sign. 'This gardenia will make you feel important all day long for 10 cents.' All at once his sales began to increase."

In our society today, most people feel isolated. The strong sense of community that was once enjoyed by most Americans has become rare. And many people don't have the family support that was more common thirty or forty years ago. For example, evangelist Bill Glass noted, "Over 90 percent of prison inmates were told by parents while growing up, 'They're going to put you in jail.'" Instead of teaching their children to believe in themselves, some parents are tearing them down. For many people, even those who are closest to them don't believe in them. They have no one on their side. No wonder even a little thing like a flower can make a difference in how a person approaches the day.

3. MOST PEOPLE CAN TELL WHEN SOMEONE ELSE HAS FAITH IN THEM

People's instincts are pretty good at knowing when others have faith in them. They can sense if your belief is genuine or phony. And truly having faith in someone can change his or her life.

In his book *Move Ahead with Possibility Thinking*, my friend Robert Schuller, pastor of the Crystal Cathedral in Garden Grove, California, tells a wonderful story about an incident that changed his life as a boy. It occurred when his uncle had faith in him and showed it in his words and actions:

> His car drove past the unpainted barn and stopped in a cloud of summer dust at our front gate. I ran barefooted across the splintery porch and saw my uncle Henry bound out of the car. He was tall, very handsome, and terribly alive with energy. After many years overseas in China, he was visiting our Iowa farm. He ran up to the old gate and put both of his big hands on my four-year-old shoulders. He smiled widely, ruffled my uncombed hair, and said, "Well! I guess you're

Robert! I think you are going to be a preacher some-day." That night I prayed secretly, "And dear God, make me a preacher when I grow up!" I believe that God made me a POSSIBILITY THINKER then and there.

Always remember that your goal is not to get people to think more highly of you. It's to get them to think more highly of themselves. Have faith in them, and they will begin to do exactly that.

4. MOST PEOPLE WILL DO ANYTHING TO LIVE UP TO YOUR FAITH IN THEM

People rise or fall to meet your level of expectations for them. If you express skepticism and doubt in others, they will return your lack of confidence with mediocrity. But if you believe in them and expect them to do well, they will go the extra mile trying to do their best. And in the process, they and you benefit. John H. Spalding expressed the thought this way: "Those who believe in our ability do more than stimulate us. They create for us an atmosphere in which it becomes easier to succeed."

HOW TO BECOME A BELIEVER IN PEOPLE

I'm fortunate because I grew up in a positive, affirming environment. As a result, I have an easy time believing in people and expressing that belief. But I realize that not everyone had the benefit of a positive upbringing. Most people need to *learn* how to have faith in others. To build your belief in others, try using these suggestions, created using the initial letters of the word *BELIEVE.*

Believe in Them Before They Succeed

Everyone loves a winner. It's easy to have faith in people who have already proved themselves. It's much tougher to believe in people *before* they have proved themselves. But that is the key to motivating people to reach their potential. You have to believe in them first, before they become successful, and sometimes before you can persuade them to believe in themselves.

Some people in your life desperately want to believe in themselves but have little hope. As you interact with them, remember the motto of French World War I hero Marshal Ferdinand Foch: "There are no hopeless situations; there are only men and women who have grown hopeless about them." Every person has seeds of greatness within, even though they may currently be dormant. But when you believe in people, you water the seeds and give them the chance to grow.

Emphasize Their Strengths

Many people mistakenly think that to build relationships and be influential, they have to be an "authority" and point out others' deficiencies. People who try that approach become like Lucy from the comic strip *Peanuts* by Charles Schulz. In one strip Lucy told poor Charlie Brown, "You're in the shadow of your own goal posts! You are a miscue! You are three putts on the eighteenth green! You are a seven-ten split in the tenth frame. . . . You are a missed free throw, a shanked nine iron and a called third strike! Do you understand? Have I made myself clear?" That's hardly a way to positively impact the life of another person!

The road to building positive relationships lies in exactly the opposite direction. The best way to show people your faith in them and motivate them is to focus your attention on their strengths. According to author and advertising executive Bruce Barton, "Nothing splendid has ever been achieved except by those who dared believe that something inside them was superior to circumstances." By emphasizing people's strengths, you're helping them believe that they possess what they need to succeed.

BELIEVING IN PEOPLE BEFORE THEY HAVE PROVED THEMSELVES IS THE KEY TO MOTIVATING PEOPLE TO REACH THEIR POTENTIAL.

Praise them for what they do well, both privately and publicly. Tell them how much you appreciate their positive qualities and their skills. And anytime you have the opportunity to compliment and praise them in the presence of their family and close friends, do it.

LIST THEIR PAST SUCCESSES

Even when you emphasize people's strengths, they may need further encouragement to show them you believe in them and to get them motivated. Entrepreneur Mary Kay Ash, founder of Mary Kay cosmetics, advised, "Everyone has an invisible sign hanging from his neck saying, 'Make me feel important!' Never forget this message when working with people." One of the best ways to do that is to help people remember their past successes.

The account of David and Goliath presents a classic example of how past successes can help a person have faith in himself. You may remember the story from the Bible. A nine-foot-tall Philistine champion named Goliath stood before the army of Israel and taunted them every day for forty days, daring them to send out a warrior to face him. On the fortieth day a young shepherd named David came to the front lines to deliver food to his brothers, who were in Israel's army. While he was there, he witnessed the giant's contemptuous display of taunts and challenges. David was so infuriated that he told King Saul he wanted to face the giant in battle. Here's what happened next:

Saul replied, "You are not able to go out against this Philistine and fight him; you are only a boy, and he has been a fighting man from his youth." But David said to Saul, "Your servant has been keeping his father's sheep. When a lion or a bear came and carried off a sheep from the flock, I went after it, struck it and rescued the sheep from its mouth. When it turned on me, I seized it by its hair, struck it and killed it. Your servant has killed both the lion and the bear. . . . The LORD who delivered me from the paw of the lion and the paw of the bear will deliver me from the hand of this Philistine."[1]

David looked back on his past successes, and he had confidence in his future actions. And of course, when he faced the giant, he felled him like a tree, using nothing but a rock and sling. And when he cut off Goliath's head his success inspired his fellow countrymen; they routed the Philistine army.

Not everyone has the natural ability to recognize past successes and draw confidence from them. Some people need help. If you can show others that they have done well in the past and help them see that their past victories have paved the way for future success, they'll be better able to move into action. Listing past successes helps others believe in themselves.

Instill Confidence When They Fail

When you have encouraged people and put your faith in them, and they begin to believe they can succeed in life, they soon reach a critical crossroads. The first time or two that they fail—and they will fail because it's a part of life—they have two choices. They can give in or go on.

Some people are resilient and willing to keep trying in order to succeed, even when they don't see immediate progress. But others aren't that determined. Some will collapse at the first sign of trouble. To give them a push and inspire them, you need to keep showing your confidence in them, even when they're making mistakes or doing poorly.

One of the ways to do that is to tell about your past troubles and traumas. Sometimes people think that if you're currently successful, you have always been that way. They don't realize that you have had your share of flops, failures, and fumbles. Show them that success is a journey—a process, not a destination. When they realize that you have failed and yet still managed to succeed, they'll realize that it's okay to fail. And their confidence will remain intact. They will learn to think the way baseball legend Babe Ruth did when he said, "Never let the fear of striking out get in the way."

EXPERIENCE SOME WINS TOGETHER

It's not enough just knowing failure is a part of moving forward in life. To really become motivated to succeed, people need to believe they can win.

Winning is motivation. Novelist David Ambrose acknowledged this truth: "If you have the will to win, you have achieved half your success; if you don't, you have achieved half your failure." Coming alongside others to help them experience some wins with you gives them reasons to believe they will succeed. And in the process, they sense victory. That's when incredible things begin to happen in their lives.

To help people believe they can achieve victory, put them in a position to experience small successes. Encourage them to perform tasks or take on responsibilities you know that they can handle and do well. And give them the assistance they need to succeed. In time as their confidence grows, they will take on more difficult challenges, but they will be able to face them with confidence and competence because of the positive track record they're developing.

VISUALIZE THEIR FUTURE SUCCESS

An experiment performed with laboratory rats measured their motivation to live under different circumstances. Scientists dropped a rat into a jar of water that had been placed in total darkness, and they timed how long the animal would continue swimming before it gave up and allowed itself to drown. They found that the rat lasted little more than three minutes.

Then they dropped another rat into the same kind of jar, but instead of placing it in total darkness, they allowed a ray of light to shine into it. Under those circumstances, the rat kept swimming for thirty-six hours. That's more than seven hundred times longer than the one in the dark! Because the rat could see, it continued to have hope.

If that is true of laboratory animals, think of how strong the effect of visualization can be on people, who are capable of higher reasoning. It's been said that a person can live forty days without food, four days without water, four minutes without air, but only four seconds without hope. Each time you cast a vision for others and paint a picture of their future success, you build them up, motivate them, and give them reasons to keep going.

Expect a New Level of Living

German statesman Konrad Adenauer observed: "We all live under the same sky, but we don't all have the same horizon." Make it your goal to help others see beyond today and their current circumstances and dream big dreams. When you put your faith in people, you help them expand their horizons and motivate them to move to a whole new level of living.

Putting your faith in others involves taking a chance. But the rewards outweigh the risks. Robert Louis Stevenson said, "To be what we are, and to become what we are capable of becoming, is the only end of life." When you put your faith in others, you help them reach their potential. You become an important relationship in their lives—and they in yours.

4

HOW CAN I CONNECT WITH PEOPLE?

Always remember, the heart comes before the head.

I love communicating. It's one of my passions. Although I've spent more than thirty years speaking professionally, I'm always looking for ways to grow and keep improving in that area.

THE AUDIENCE'S BEST FRIEND

No doubt you've heard of Elizabeth Dole. She is a lawyer by trade, was a cabinet member in the Reagan and Bush administrations, and was the president of the American Red Cross. She is a marvelous communicator. Her particular gift, which I witnessed in San Jose one day, was making me and everyone else in her audience feel as though she was really our friend. She made me glad I was there. The bottom line is that she really knows how to connect with people.

In 1996, she demonstrated that ability to the whole country when she spoke at the Republican National Convention.

If you watched it on television, you know what I'm talking about. When Elizabeth Dole walked out into the audience that night, they felt that she was their best friend. She was able to develop an amazing connection with them. I also felt that connection, even though I was sitting in my living room at home watching her on television. Once she finished her talk, I would have followed her anywhere.

BOB NEVER MADE THE CONNECTION

Also speaking at that convention was Bob Dole, Elizabeth's husband—not surprising since he was the Republican nominee for the presidential race. Anyone who watched would have observed a remarkable difference between the communication abilities of the two speakers. Where Elizabeth was warm and approachable, Bob appeared stern and distant. Throughout the campaign, he never seemed to be able to connect with the people.

Many factors come into play in the election of a president of the United States, but not least among them is the ability of a candidate to connect with his audience. A lot has been written about the Kennedy-Nixon debates of the 1960 election. One of the reasons John F. Kennedy succeeded was that he was able to make the television audience feel connected to him. The same kind of connection developed between Ronald Reagan and his audiences. And in the 1992 election, Bill Clinton worked extremely hard to develop a sense of connection with the American people— to do it he even appeared on the talk show *Arsenio* and played the saxophone.

YOU CAN'T MOVE PEOPLE TO ACTION UNLESS YOU FIRST MOVE THEM WITH EMOTION. THE HEART COMES BEFORE THE HEAD.

I believe Bob Dole is a good man. But I also know he never connected with the people. Ironically, after the presidential race was over, he appeared on *Saturday Night Live,* a show that made fun of him during the entire campaign, implying that he was humorless and out of touch. On the show Dole came across as relaxed, approachable, and able to make fun of himself. And he was a hit with the audience. He had finally connected.

THE HEART COMES FIRST

You first have to touch people's hearts before you ask them for a hand. All great communicators recognize this truth and act on it almost instinctively. You can't move people to action unless you first move them with emotion. The heart comes before the head.

An outstanding orator and African-American leader of the nineteenth century was Frederick Douglass. It's said that he had a remarkable ability to connect with people and move their hearts when he spoke. Historian Lerone Bennett said of Douglass, "He could make people *laugh* at a slave owner preaching the duties of Christian obedience; could make them *see* the humiliation of a Black maiden ravished by a brutal slave owner; could make them *hear* the sobs of a mother separated from her child. Through him, people could cry, curse, and *feel;* through him they could *live* slavery."

CONNECT IN PUBLIC AND PRIVATE

Connecting with people isn't something that needs to happen only when communicating to groups of people. It needs to happen with individuals. And the stronger the relationship between individuals, the more beneficial it will be and the more likely the follower will want to help the leader. That is one of the most important principles I've taught my staff over the years. My staff used to groan every time I would say, "People don't care how much you know until they know how much you care," but they also knew that it was true. You develop credibility with people when you connect with them and show that you genuinely want to help them.

CONNECT WITH PEOPLE ONE AT A TIME

A key to connecting with others is recognizing that even in a group, you have to relate to people as individuals. General Norman Schwarzkopf remarked, "I have seen competent leaders who stood in front of a platoon and all they saw was a platoon. But great leaders stand in front of a platoon and see it as 44 individuals, each of whom has aspirations, each of whom wants to live, each of whom wants to do good."[1] That's the only way to connect with people.

PUT A "10" ON EVERY PERSON'S HEAD

One of the best things you can do for people is to expect the best of them. I call it putting a "10" on everyone's head. It helps others think more highly of themselves, and at the same time, it also helps you. According to Jacques Wiesel, "A survey of one hundred self-made millionaires showed only one common denominator. These highly successful men and women could only see the good in people."

Benjamin Disraeli understood and practiced this concept, and it was one of the secrets of his charisma. He once said, "The greatest good you can do for another is not just to share your riches but to reveal to him his own." If you appreciate others, encourage them, and help them reach their potential, they will connect with you.

THE TOUGHER THE CHALLENGE, THE GREATER THE CONNECTION

Never underestimate the power of building relationships with people. If you've ever studied the lives of notable military commanders, you have probably noticed that the best ones understood how to connect with people. I once read that during World War I in France, General Douglas MacArthur told a battalion commander before a daring charge, "Major, when the signal comes to go over the top, I want you to go first, before your men. If you do, they'll follow." Then MacArthur removed the Distinguished Service Cross from his uniform and pinned it on the major. He had, in effect, awarded him for heroism before asking him to exhibit it. And of course, the major led his men, they followed him over the top, and they achieved their objective.

THE RESULT OF CONNECTION IN THE WORKPLACE

When a leader has done the work to connect with his people, you can see it in the way the organization functions. Among employees there are incredible loyalty and a strong work ethic. The vision of the leader becomes the aspiration of the people. The impact is incredible.

You can also see the results in other ways. On Boss's Day in 1994, a full-page ad appeared in *USA Today*. It was contracted and paid for by the employees of Southwest Airlines, and it was addressed to Herb Kelleher, the company's CEO:

Thanks, Herb
For remembering every one of our names.
For supporting the Ronald McDonald House.
For helping load baggage on Thanksgiving.
For giving everyone a kiss (and we mean everyone).
For listening.
For running the only profitable major airline.
For singing at our holiday party.
For singing only once a year.
For letting us wear shorts and sneakers to work.
For golfing at The LUV Classic with only one club.
For outtalking Sam Donaldson.
For riding your Harley Davidson into Southwest
    Headquarters.
For being a friend, not just a boss.
Happy Boss's Day from Each One of Your 16,000
    Employees.[2]

A display of affection like that occurs only when a leader has worked hard to connect with his people.

Don't ever underestimate the importance of building relational bridges between yourself and. others around you. There's an old saying: To lead yourself, use your head; to lead others, use your heart. Always touch a person's heart before you ask him for a hand.

5

How Can I Become
a Better Listener?

Treat every person as if he or she were the
most important person in the world.

Edgar Watson Howe once joked, "No man would listen to you talk if he didn't know it was his turn next." Unfortunately, that accurately describes the way too many people approach communication—they're too busy waiting for their turn to really listen to others. But successful people understand the incredible value of becoming a good listener.

The ability to skillfully listen is the foundation to building positive relationships with others. When Lyndon B. Johnson was a junior senator from Texas, he kept a sign on his office wall that read, "You ain't learnin' nothin' when you're doin' all the talkin'." And Woodrow Wilson, the twenty-eighth American president, once said, "The ear of the leader must ring with the voices of the people."

THE VALUE OF LISTENING

Consider these benefits to listening:

LISTENING SHOWS RESPECT

A mistake that people often make in communicating is trying very hard to impress the other person. They try to make themselves appear smart, witty, or entertaining. But if you want to relate well to others, you have to be willing to focus on what they have to offer. Be *impressed* and *interested*, not *impressive* and *interesting*. Poet-philosopher Ralph Waldo Emerson acknowledged, "Every man I meet is in some way my superior, and I can learn of him." Remember that and listen, and the lines of communication will really open up.

LISTENING BUILDS RELATIONSHIPS

Dale Carnegie, author of *How to Win Friends and Influence People*, advised, "You can make more friends in two weeks by becoming a good listener than you can in two years trying to get people interested in you." Carnegie was incredibly gifted at understanding relationships. He recognized that people who are self-focused and who talk about themselves and their concerns all the time rarely develop strong relationships with others. David Schwartz noted in *The Magic of Thinking Big*, "Big people monopolize the listening. Small people monopolize the talking."

By becoming a good listener, you are able to connect with others on more levels and develop stronger, deeper relationships because you are meeting a need. Author C. Neil Strait pointed out that "everyone needs someone who he feels really listens to him." When you become that important listener, you help that person.

LISTENING INCREASES KNOWLEDGE

Wilson Mizner said, "A good listener is not only popular everywhere, but after a while he knows something." It's amazing how much you can learn about your friends and family, your job, the organization you work in, and yourself when you decide to really listen to others. But not everyone clues into this benefit. For example, I once heard a story about a tennis pro who was giving a lesson to a new student. After watching the novice take several swings at the tennis ball, the pro stopped him and suggested ways he could improve his stroke. But each time he did, the student interrupted him, gave a different opinion of the problem, and stated how it should be solved. After several interruptions, the pro began to nod his head in agreement.

When the lesson ended, a woman who had been watching said to the pro, "Why did you go along with that arrogant man's stupid suggestions?"

The pro smiled and replied, "I learned a long time ago that

it is a waste of time to try to sell real *answers* to anyone who just wants to buy *echoes*."

Beware of putting yourself into a position where you think you know all the answers. Anytime you do, you'll be putting yourself in danger. It's almost impossible to think of yourself as "the expert" and continue growing and learning at the same time. All great learners are great listeners.

One common problem as people gain more authority is that they often listen to others less and less, especially the people who report to them. While it's true that the higher you go, the less you are required to listen to others, it's also true that your need for good listening skills increases. The farther you get from the front lines, the more you have to depend on others to get reliable information. Only if you develop good listening skills early, and then continue to use them, will you be able to gather the information you need to succeed.

As you proceed through life and become more successful, don't lose sight of your need to keep growing and improving yourself. And remember, a deaf ear is evidence of a closed mind.

LISTENING GENERATES IDEAS

Good companies have a reputation for listening to their people. Brinker International, owner of Chili's, On the

Border, Romano's Macaroni Grill, and other restaurant chains, is one of the nation's best-run food service chains according to *Restaurants and Institutions* magazine. Almost 80 percent of its restaurants' menu items have come from suggestions made by unit managers.

What's good for effective companies is good for individuals. When you consistently listen to others, you never suffer for ideas. People love to contribute, especially when their leader shares the credit with them. If you give people opportunities to share their thoughts, and you listen with an open mind, there will always be a flow of new ideas. And even if you hear ideas that won't work, just listening to them can often spark other creative thoughts in you and others. You'll never know how close you are to a million-dollar idea unless you're willing to listen.

Listening Builds Loyalty

A funny thing happens when you don't make a practice of listening to people. They find others who will. Anytime employees, spouses, colleagues, children, or friends no longer believe they are being listened to, they seek out people who will give them what they want. Sometimes the consequences can be disastrous: the end of a friendship, lack of authority at work, lessened parental influence, or the breakdown of a marriage.

On the other hand, practicing good listening skills draws people to you. Everyone loves a good listener and is attracted to him or her. And if you consistently listen to others, valuing them and what they have to offer, they are likely to develop a strong loyalty to you, even when your authority with them is unofficial or informal.

LISTENING IS A GREAT WAY TO HELP OTHERS AND YOURSELF

Roger G. Imhoff urged, "Let others confide in you. It may not help you, but it will surely help them." At first glance, listening to others may appear to benefit only them. But when you become a good listener, you put yourself in a position to help yourself too. You have the ability to develop strong relationships, gather valuable information, and increase your understanding of yourself and others.

HOW TO DEVELOP LISTENING SKILLS

To become a good listener, you have to want to hear. But you also need some skills to help you. Here are nine suggestions to help you become a better listener:

1. LOOK AT THE SPEAKER

The whole listening process begins with giving the other person your undivided attention. As you interact with someone, don't catch up on other work, shuffle papers, do the dishes, or watch television. Set aside the time to focus only on the other person. And if you don't have the time at that moment, then schedule it as soon as you can.

2. Don't Interrupt

Most people react badly to being interrupted. It makes them feel disrespected. And according to Robert L. Montgomery, author of *Listening Made Easy*, "It's just as rude to step on other people's ideas as it is to step on their toes."

People who tend to interrupt others generally do so for one of these reasons:

- They don't place enough value on what the other person has to say.

- They want to impress others by showing how smart and intuitive they are.

- They're too excited by the conversation to let the other person finish talking.

If you are in the habit of interrupting other people, examine your motives and determine to make a change. Give people the time they need to express themselves. And don't feel that one of you has to speak all the time. Periods of silence can give you a chance to reflect on what's been said so that you can respond appropriately.

3. FOCUS ON UNDERSTANDING

Have you ever noticed how quickly most people forget the things they hear? Studies at institutions such as Michigan State, Ohio State, Florida State, and the University of Minnesota indicate that most people can recall only 50 percent of what they hear immediately after hearing it. And as the time passes, their ability to remember continues to drop. By the next day, their retention is usually down to 25 percent.

One way to combat that tendency is to aim for understanding rather than just remembering the facts. Lawyer, lecturer, and author Herb Cohen emphasized, "Effective listening requires more than hearing the words transmitted. It demands that you find meaning and understanding in what is being said. After all, meanings are not in words, but in people."

4. DETERMINE THE NEED AT THE MOMENT

A lot of men and women find themselves in conflict because they occasionally communicate at cross-purposes. They neglect to determine the need of the other person at the moment of interaction. Men usually want to fix any problems they discuss; their need is resolution. Women, on the other hand, are more likely to tell about a problem simply to share it; they neither request nor desire solutions. Anytime you can determine the current need of the people you're communicating with, you can put whatever they say into the appropriate context. And you will be better able to understand them.

IF YOU SHOW PEOPLE HOW MUCH YOU CARE AND ASK QUESTIONS IN A NONTHREATENING WAY, YOU'LL BE AMAZED BY HOW MUCH THEY'LL TELL YOU.

---

5. CHECK YOUR EMOTIONS

Most people carry around emotional baggage that causes them to react to certain people or situations. Sigmund Freud states, "A man with a toothache cannot be in love," meaning that the toothache doesn't allow him to notice anything other than his pain. Similarly, anytime a person has an ax to grind, the words of others are drowned out by the sound of the grindstone.

Anytime that you become highly emotional when listening to another person, check your emotions—especially if your reaction seems to be stronger than the situation warrants. You don't want to make an unsuspecting person the recipient of your venting. Besides, even if your reactions are not due to an event from your past, you should always allow others to finish explaining their points of view, ideas, or convictions before offering your own.

6. SUSPEND YOUR JUDGMENT

Have you ever begun listening to another person tell a story and started to respond to it before he or she was finished? Just about everyone has. But the truth is that you can't jump to conclusions and be a good listener at the same time. As you talk to others, wait to hear the whole story before you respond. If you don't, you may miss the most important thing they intend to say.

7. SUM UP AT MAJOR INTERVALS

Experts agree that listening is most effective when it's active. John H. Melchinger suggests, "Comment on what you hear, and individualize your comments. For example, you can say, 'Cheryl, that's obviously very important to you.' It will help keep you on track as a listener. Get beyond, 'That's interesting.' If you train yourself to comment meaningfully, the speaker will know you are listening and may offer further information."

A technique for active listening is to sum up what the other person says at major intervals. As the speaker finishes one subject, paraphrase his or her main points or ideas before going on to the next one, and verify that you have gotten the right message. Doing that reassures the person and helps you stay focused on what he or she is trying to communicate.

8. Ask Questions for Clarity

Have you ever noticed that top reporters are excellent listeners? Take someone like Barbara Walters, for example. She looks at the speaker, focuses on understanding, suspends judgment, and sums up what the person has to say. People trust her and seem to be willing to tell her just about anything. But she practices another skill that helps her to gather more information and increase her understanding of the person she is interviewing. She asks good questions.

If you want to become an effective listener, become a good reporter—not a stick-the-microphone-in-your-face-and-bark-questions-at-you reporter, but someone who gently asks follow-up questions and seeks clarification. If you show people how much you care and ask in a nonthreatening way, you'll be amazed by how much they'll tell you.

9. Always Make Listening Your Priority

The last thing to remember when developing your listening skills is to make listening a priority, no matter how busy you become or how far you rise in your organization. A remarkable example of a busy executive who made time for listening was the late Sam Walton, founder of Wal-Mart and one of the richest men in America. He believed in listening to what people had to say, especially his employees. He once flew his plane to Mt. Pleasant, Texas, landed, and gave instructions to his copilot to meet him about one hundred miles down the road. He then rode in a Wal-Mart truck just so that he could chat with the driver. We should all give listening that kind of priority.

Many people take for granted the ability to listen. Most people consider listening to be easy, and they view themselves as pretty good listeners. But while it's true that most people are able to hear, fewer are capable of really listening. However, it's never too late to become a good listener. It can change your life—and the lives of the people in your life.

PART III

THE GROWTH
OF RELATIONSHIPS

HOW CAN I BUILD
TRUST WITH OTHERS?

*When your words and actions match,
people know they can trust you.*

I n his best-selling book *The Seven Habits of Highly Effective People*, Stephen Covey wrote about the importance of integrity to a person's success:

> If I try to use human influence strategies and tactics of how to get other people to do what I want, to work better, to be more motivated, to like me and each other—while my character is fundamentally flawed, marked by duplicity or insincerity—then, in the long run, I cannot be successful. My duplicity will breed distrust, and everything I do—even using so-called good human relations techniques—will be perceived as manipulative.
>
> It simply makes no difference how good the rhetoric is or even how good the intentions are; if there is little or no

trust, there is no foundation or permanent success. Only basic goodness gives life to technique.[1]

Integrity is crucial for business and personal success. A joint study conducted by the UCLA Graduate School of Management and Korn/Ferry International of New York City surveyed 1,300 senior executives. Seventy-one percent of them said that integrity was the quality most needed to succeed in business. And a study by the Center for Creative Research discovered that though many errors and obstacles can be overcome by a person who wants to rise to the top of an organization, that person is almost never able to move up in the organization if he compromises his integrity by betraying a trust.

INTEGRITY IS ABOUT THE SMALL THINGS

Integrity is important to building relationships. And it is the foundation upon which many other qualities for success are built, such as respect, dignity, and trust. If the foundation of integrity is weak or fundamentally flawed, then success becomes impossible. As author and friend Cheryl Biehl points out, "One of the realities of life is that if you can't trust a person at all points, you can't truly trust him or her at any point." Even people who are able to hide their lack of integrity for a period of time will eventually experience failure, and their relationships will suffer.

It's crucial to maintain integrity by taking care of the little things. Many people misunderstand that. They think they can do whatever they want when it comes to the small things because they believe that as long as they don't have any major lapses, they're doing well. But ethical principles are not flexible. A little white lie is still a lie. Theft is theft—whether it's $1, $1,000, or $1 million. Integrity commits itself to character over personal gain, to people over things, to service over power, to principle over convenience, to the long view over the immediate.

Nineteenth-century clergyman Philips Brooks maintained, "Character is made in the small moments of our lives." Anytime you break a moral principle, you create a small crack in the foundation of your integrity. And when times get tough, it becomes harder to act with integrity, not easier. Character isn't created in a crisis; it only comes to light. Everything you have done in the past—and the things you have neglected to do—come to a head when you're under pressure.

Developing and maintaining integrity require constant attention. Josh Weston, former chairman and CEO of Automatic Data Processing, Inc., says, "I've always tried to live with the following simple rule: 'Don't do what you wouldn't feel comfortable reading about in the newspapers the next day.'" That's a good standard all of us should keep.

INTEGRITY IS AN INSIDE JOB

One of the reasons many people struggle with integrity issues is that they tend to look outside themselves to explain any deficiencies in character. But the development of integrity is an inside job. Take a look at the following three truths about integrity that go against common thinking:

1. INTEGRITY IS NOT DETERMINED BY CIRCUMSTANCES

It's true that our upbringing and circumstances affect who we are, especially when we are young. But the older we get, the greater the number of choices we make—for good or bad. Two people can grow up in the same environment, even in the same household, and one will have integrity and the other won't. Your circumstances are as responsible for your character as a mirror is for your looks. Who you see only reflects who you are.

2. INTEGRITY IS NOT BASED ON CREDENTIALS

In ancient times, brick makers, engravers, and other artisans used a symbol to mark the things they created. The symbol that each one used was his "character." The value of the work was in proportion to the skill with which the object was made. And only if the quality of the work was high was the character esteemed. In other words, the quality of the person and his work gave value to his credentials. If the work was good, so was the character. If it was bad, then the character was viewed as poor.

The same is true for us today. Character comes from who we are. But some people would like to be judged not by who they are, but by the titles they have earned or the position they hold, regardless of the nature of their character. Their desire is to influence others by the weight of their credentials rather than the strength of their character. But credentials can never accomplish what character can. Look at some differences between the two:

CREDENTIALS	CHARACTER
Are transient	Is permanent
Turn the focus to rights	Keeps the focus on responsibilities
Add value to only one person	Adds value to many people
Look to past accomplishments	Builds a legacy for the future

| Often evoke jealousy in others | Generates respect and integrity |
| Can only get you in the door | Keeps you there |

No number of titles, degrees, offices, designations, awards, licenses, or other credentials can substitute for basic, honest integrity when it comes to the power of influencing others.

3. INTEGRITY IS NOT TO BE CONFUSED WITH REPUTATION

Certainly a good reputation is valuable. King Solomon of ancient Israel stated, "A good name is more desirable than great riches."[2] But a good reputation exists because it is a reflection of a person's character. If a good reputation is like gold, then having integrity is like owning the mine. Worry less about what others think, and give your attention to your inner character. D. L. Moody wrote, "If I take care of my character, my reputation will take care of itself."

If you struggle with maintaining your integrity, and you're doing all the right things on the *outside*—but you're still getting the wrong results—something is wrong and still needs to be changed on the *inside*. Look at the questions on the following page. They may help you nail down areas that need attention.

Questions to Help You Measure Your Integrity

1. How well do I treat people if I gain nothing?

2. Am I transparent with others?

3. Do I role-play based on the person(s) I'm with?

4. Am I the same person in the spotlight as I am when I'm alone?

5. Do I quickly admit wrongdoing without being pressed to do so?

6. Do I put people ahead of my personal agenda?

7. Do I have an unchanging standard for moral decisions, or do circumstances determine my choices?

8. Do I make difficult decisions, even when they have a personal cost attached to them?

9. When I have something to say about people, do I talk *to* them or *about* them?

10. Am I accountable to at least one other person for what I think, say, and do?

Don't be too quick to respond to the questions. If character development is a serious area of need in your life, your tendency may be to skim through the questions, giving answers that describe how you wish you were rather than who you actually are. Take some time to reflect on each question, honestly considering it before answering. Then work on the areas where you're having the most trouble.

INTEGRITY IS YOUR BEST FRIEND

Integrity is your best friend. It will never betray you or put you in a compromising position. It keeps your priorities right. When you're tempted to take shortcuts, it helps you to stay the right course. When others criticize you unfairly, it helps you keep going and take the high road of not striking back. And when others' criticism is valid, integrity helps you to accept what they say, learn from it, and keep growing.

IF A GOOD REPUTATION IS LIKE GOLD, THEN HAVING
INTEGRITY IS LIKE OWNING THE MINE.

Abraham Lincoln once stated, "When I lay down the reins of this administration, I want to have one friend left. And that friend is inside myself." You could almost say that

Lincoln's integrity was his best friend while he was in office because he was criticized so viciously. Here is a description of what he faced as explained by Donald T. Phillips:

> Abraham Lincoln was slandered, libeled and hated perhaps more intensely than any man ever to run for the nation's highest office. . . . He was publicly called just about every name imaginable by the press of his day, including a grotesque baboon, a third-rate country lawyer who once split rails and now splits the Union, a coarse vulgar joker, a dictator, an ape, a buffoon, and others. The *Illinois State Register* labeled him "the craftiest and most dishonest politician that ever disgraced an office in America. . . ." Severe and unjust criticism did not subside after Lincoln took the oath of office, nor did it come only from Southern sympathizers. It came from within the Union itself, from Congress, from some factions within the Republican party, and initially, from within his own cabinet. As president, Lincoln learned that, no matter what he did, there were going to be people who would not be pleased.[3]

Through it all, Lincoln was a man of principle. And as Thomas Jefferson wisely said, "God grant that men of principle shall be our principal men."

INTEGRITY IS YOUR FRIENDS' BEST FRIEND

Integrity is your best friend. And it's also one of the best friends that your friends will ever have. When the people around you know that you're a person of integrity, they know that you want to influence them because of the opportunity to add value to their lives. They don't have to worry about your motives.

If you're a basketball fan, you probably remember Red Auerbach. He was the president and general manager of the Boston Celtics from 1967 to 1987. He truly understood how integrity adds value to others, especially when people are working together on a team. And he had a method of recruiting that was different from that of most NBA team leaders. When he reviewed a prospective player for the Celtics, his primary concern was the young man's character. While others focused almost entirely on statistics and individual performance, Auerbach wanted to know about a player's attitude. He figured that the way to win was to find players who would give their best work for the benefit of the team. A player who had outstanding ability but whose character was weak or whose desire was to promote only himself was not really an asset.

It has been said that you don't really know people until you have observed them when they interact with a child, when the car has a flat tire, when the boss is away, and when they think no one will ever know. But people with integrity never have to worry about that. No matter where they are, who they are with, or what kind of situation they find themselves in, they are consistent and live by their principles.

BECOME A PERSON OF INTEGRITY

In the end, you can bend your actions to conform to your principles, or you can bend your principles to conform to your actions. It's a choice you have to make. If you want to be successful, then you better choose the path of integrity because all other roads ultimately lead to ruin.

To become a person of integrity, you need to go back to the fundamentals. You may have to make some tough choices, but they'll be worth it.

COMMIT YOURSELF TO HONESTY, RELIABILITY, AND CONFIDENTIALITY

Integrity begins with a specific, conscious decision. If you wait until a moment of crisis before settling your integrity issues, you set yourself up to fail. Choose today to live by a strict moral code, and determine to stick with it no matter what happens.

DECIDE AHEAD OF TIME THAT YOU DON'T HAVE A PRICE

President George Washington perceived that "few men have the virtue to withstand the highest bidder." Some people can be bought because they haven't settled the money issue before the moment of temptation. The best way to guard yourself against a breach in integrity is to make a decision today that you won't sell your integrity: not for power, revenge, pride, or money—any amount of money.

EACH DAY, DO WHAT YOU SHOULD DO BEFORE WHAT YOU WANT TO DO

A big part of integrity is following through consistently on your responsibilities. Our friend Zig Ziglar says, "When you do the things you have to do when you have to do them, the day will come when you can do the things you want to do when you want to do them." Psychologist-philosopher William James stated the idea more strongly: "Everybody ought to do at least two things each day that he hates to do, just for the practice."

With integrity, you can experience freedom. Not only are you less likely to be enslaved by the stress that comes from bad choices, debt, deceptiveness, and other negative character issues, but you are free to influence others and add value to them in an incredible way. And your integrity opens the door for you to experience continued success.

If you know what you stand for and act accordingly, people can trust you. You are a model of the character and consistency that other people admire and want to emulate. And you've laid a good foundation, one that makes it possible for you to build positive relationships.

WHAT IS MY MOST IMPORTANT RELATIONSHIP?

Succeed at home, and all other relationships become easier.

Did you know that according to the Bureau of Labor Statistics, families dissolve at a greater rate in the United States than in any other major industrialized country? And we also lead in the number of fathers absent from the home. U.S. divorce laws are the most permissible in the world, and people are using them at an alarming rate.[1] To some people, marriages and families have become acceptable casualties in the pursuit of success.

But many people are now realizing that the hope of happiness at the expense of breaking up a family is an illusion. You can't give up your marriage or neglect your children and gain true success. Building and maintaining strong families benefit us in every way, including in helping us become successful. Family life expert Nick Stinnet asserted more than a decade ago, "When you have a strong family life, you receive the message that you are loved, cared for and important. *The*

*positive intake of love, affection, and respect . . . gives you inner
resources to deal with life more successfully"* (emphasis added).

WORKING TO STAY TOGETHER

Fairly early in our marriage, Margaret and I realized that in
my career, I would often have the opportunity to travel. And
we decided that any time I got the chance to go someplace
interesting or to attend an event that we knew would be exciting, she would come along with me, even when it was difficult financially. We've done a pretty good job of following
through on that commitment over the years.

Margaret and I, with our kids Elizabeth and Joel Porter,
have been to the capitals of Europe, the jungles of South
America, the teeming cities of Korea, the rugged outback of
Australia, and on safari in South Africa. We've met wonderful
people of every race and a multitude of nationalities. We've had
the chance to see and do things that will remain in our memories for the rest of our lives. I decided early on, what would
it profit me to gain the whole world and lose my family?

I know that I wouldn't have experienced any measure of
success in life without Margaret. But my gratitude to her and
the children doesn't come from what they've brought me. It
comes from who they are to me. When I reach the end of my
days, I don't want Margaret, Elizabeth, or Joel Porter to say

that I was a good author, speaker, pastor, or leader. My desire is that the kids think I'm a good father and that Margaret thinks I'm a good husband. That's what matters most. It's the measure of true success.

STEPS TO BUILDING A STRONG FAMILY

Good marriages and strong families are joys, but they don't just happen on their own. Dr. R. C. Adams, who studied thousands of marriages over a ten-year period, found that only 17 percent of the unions he studied could be considered truly happy. And Jarle Brors, former director of the Institute of Marriage and Family Relations in Washington, D.C., said, "We are finally realizing that we have to go back to the basics in order to reestablish the type of families that give us the type of security that children can grow up in." If we want to have solid families and healthy marriages, we have to work hard to create them.

If you have a family—or you intend to have one in the future—take a look at the following guidelines. They have helped to develop the Maxwell family, and I believe they can help you to strengthen yours.

EXPRESS APPRECIATION FOR EACH OTHER

I once heard someone joke that home is the place where family members go when they are tired of being nice to other people. Unfortunately, some homes seem to work that way. A salesman spends his day treating his clients with the utmost kindness, often in the face of rejection, in order to build his business, but he is rude to his wife when he comes home. Or a doctor spends the day being caring and compassionate with her patients, but she comes home exhausted and blows up with her children.

To build a strong family, you have to make your home a supportive environment. Psychologist William James observed, "In every person from the cradle to the grave, there is a deep craving to be appreciated." Feeling appreciated brings out the best in people. And when that appreciation comes in the home and is coupled with acceptance, love, and encouragement, the bonds between family members grow, and the home becomes a safe haven for everyone.

WHAT WOULD IT PROFIT ME TO GAIN THE
WHOLE WORLD AND LOSE MY FAMILY?

I've heard that for every negative remark to a family member, it takes four positive statements to counteract the damage. That's why it's so important to focus on the positive aspects of each other's personality and express unconditional love for each other, both verbally and nonverbally. Then the home becomes a positive environment for everyone.

STRUCTURE YOUR LIVES TO SPEND TIME TOGETHER

It's been said that the American home has become a domestic cloverleaf upon which family members pass each other while en route to a multitude of places and activities. That seems to be true. When I was a kid, I spent a lot of time with my parents, brother, and sister. We went on family vacations, usually in the car. As a parent, it's been harder for me to keep that tradition alive. We've been good about planning and taking vacations together, but sometimes we've had to be creative to have time together. For example, when the children were younger, I always tried to drive them to school in the morning to spend some time with them. But with all the things going on in our busy lives, we found that the only way to get time together was to plan it carefully.

Every month, I spend several hours examining my travel schedule, figuring out what lessons I need to write, thinking about the projects I have to complete, and so on. And at that time, I'll plan my work for the whole month. But before I mark any dates for work, I write in all the important dates for family activities. I'll block out time for birthdays, anniversaries, ball games, theater performances, graduation ceremonies, concerts, and romantic dinners. And I'll also schedule special one-on-one time with Margaret and each of the kids so that we can continue to build our relationships. Then once those are set, I'll plan my work schedule around them. I've done this for years, and it's been the only thing that's prevented my work from squeezing my family out of the schedule. I've found that if I don't strategically structure my life to spend time with my family, it won't happen.

DEAL WITH CRISIS IN A POSITIVE WAY

Every family experiences problems, but not all families respond to them in the same way. And that often separates a family that's close from one that's barely holding together. I've noticed that some people pursuing success seem to avoid the home environment. I suspect that one reason is that they are not able to handle family crisis situations well. They find it easier to try to avoid the problems altogether. But that's not a solution.

M. Scott Peck, author of *The Road Less Traveled,* has offered some remarkable insights on the subject of problems and how we handle them:

> It is in this whole process of meeting and solving problems that life has meaning. Problems are the cutting edge that distinguishes between success and failure. Problems call forth our courage and wisdom; indeed they create our courage and our wisdom. It is only because of problems that we grow mentally and spiritually. . . . It is through the pain of confronting

and resolving problems that we learn. As Benjamin Franklin said, "Those things that hurt, instruct."

If we are to grow as families and be successful at home as well as in the other areas of our lives, we must learn to cope with the difficulties we find there. Here are some strategies to help you with the problem-solving process:

- *Attack the problem, never the person.* Always try to be supportive of each other. Remember, you're all on the same side. So don't take your frustrations out on people. Instead, attack the problem.

- *Get all the facts.* Nothing can cause more damage than jumping to false conclusions during a crisis. Don't waste your emotional or physical energy chasing down a wrong problem. Before you try to find solutions, be sure you know what's really going on.

- *List all the options.* This may sound a bit analytical, but it really helps because you can look at emotional subjects with some objectivity. Besides, if you had a problem at work, you would probably be willing to go through this process. Give any family problem at least as much time and energy as you would a professional one.

- *Choose the best solution.* As you decide on a solution, always remember that people are your priority. Make your choices accordingly.

- *Look for the positives in the problem.* As Dr. Peck said, the tough things give us a chance to grow. No matter how bad things look at the moment, just about everything has something positive that comes from it.

- *Never withhold love.* No matter how bad things get or how angry you are, never withhold your love from your spouse or children. Sure, tell them how you feel. Acknowledge the problems. But continue loving family members unconditionally through it all.

This last point is the most important of all. When you feel loved and supported by your family, you can weather nearly any crisis. And you can truly enjoy success.

COMMUNICATE CONTINUALLY

An article in the *Dallas Morning News* reported that the average couple married ten years or more spends only thirty-seven minutes a week in meaningful communication. I could hardly believe it. Compare that to the fact that the average American spends almost five times longer than that watching television every day! No wonder so many marriages are in trouble. Just like anything else, good communication doesn't develop by itself. It must be developed, and that process takes time and effort. Here are some suggestions for helping you do exactly that:

- *Develop platforms for communication.* Be creative about finding reasons to talk to each other. Take walks together as a family where you can talk. Call your spouse a couple of times during the day. Meet for lunch one day a week. Offer to drive the kids to soccer practice so you can talk. Communication can happen almost anywhere.

- *Control communication killers.* The television and the telephone probably steal the most family communication time. Restrict the amount of time you give them, and you'd be amazed by how much time you have to talk.

- *Encourage honesty and transparency in conversations.* Differences of opinion are healthy and normal in a family. Encourage all family members to speak their minds, and then when they do, never criticize or ridicule them.

- *Adopt a positive communication style.* Be conscious of the way you interact with your family members. You may have adopted a style that stifles open communication. If you're in the habit of using any communication style other than a cooperative one, begin working immediately to change. You'll have to do that if you want to build your relationship with your family.

SHARE THE SAME VALUES

Today, families don't give values the same priority or attention as they once did. Boston College education professor William Kilpatrick said, "There is a myth that parents don't have the right to instill their values in their children. Once again, the standard dogma here is that children must create their own values. But of course, children have precious little chance to do that. . . . Does it make sense for parents to remain neutral bystanders when everyone else from script writers, to entertainers, to advertisers, to sex educators insist on selling their values to children?"[2]

Common values strengthen a family and are especially beneficial to children as they grow up. A study conducted by the Search Institute showed that in single-parent homes, children whose parent expresses and enforces standards thrive at twice the rate of children who don't have values promoted in a similar way.[3] And that doesn't even take into account whether the values are what we would consider positive.

The best way to get started in working toward sharing common values in your family is to identify the values you want to instill. If you're like most families, you've never done that before. But to be able to live them out, you first have to find them out. They are the three to seven things you're willing to go to the mat for.

Let me list for you the five we've identified in the Maxwell family so that you have an idea of what I'm talking about:

1. Commitment to God

2. Commitment to personal and family growth

3. Commonly shared experiences

4. Confidence in ourselves and others

5. The desire to make a contribution in life

The values you choose will undoubtedly be different from ours, but you need to identify them. If you've never done it before, set aside some time to talk about your values with your spouse and children. If your kids are older, include them in the process of identifying the values. Make it a discussion time. And never be reluctant to take on the role of model and teacher of your family's values. If you don't do it, someone else will.

BUILD YOUR MARRIAGE

Finally, if you are married, the best thing you can do to strengthen your family is to build your marriage relationship. It's certainly the best thing you can do for your spouse, but it also has an incredibly positive impact on your children. My friend Josh McDowell wisely stated, "The greatest thing a father can do for his children is to love their mother." And the greatest thing a mother can do for her children is to love their father.

A common missing ingredient in many marriages is dedication to make things work. Marriages may start because of love, but they finish because of commitment. Sexuality researcher Dr. Alfred Kinsey, who studied six thousand marriages and three thousand divorces, revealed that "there may be nothing more important in a marriage than a determination that it shall persist. With such a determination, individuals force themselves to adjust and to accept situations which would seem sufficient grounds for a breakup, if continuation of the marriage were not the prime objective." If you want to help your spouse, your children, and yourself, then become committed to building and sustaining a strong marriage.

NBA coach Pat Riley said, "Sustain a family life for a long period of time and you can sustain success for a long period of time. First things first. If your life is in order you can do whatever you want." There is definitely a correlation between family success and personal success. Not only does building strong family relationships lay the groundwork for future success, but it also gives life deeper meaning.

I believe that few people have ever been truly successful without a positive, supportive family. No matter how great people's accomplishments are, I think they're still missing something when they're working without the benefit of those close relationships. True, some people are called to be single, but they are rare. For most people, a good family helps you know your purpose and develop your potential, and it helps you enjoy the journey along the way with an intensity that isn't possible otherwise. And when it comes to sowing seeds that benefit others, who could possibly derive greater benefit from you than your own family members?

How Can I Serve and Lead People at the Same Time?

You've got to love your people more than your position.

U.S. Army General H. Norman Schwarzkopf displayed
highly successful leadership abilities in commanding
the allied troops in the Persian Gulf War, just as he had done
throughout his career, beginning in his days at West Point.

In Vietnam he turned around a battalion that was in
shambles. The First Battalion of the Sixth Infantry—known
as the "worst of the sixth"—went from laughingstock to effective fighting force and were selected to perform a more difficult mission. That turned out to be an assignment to what
Schwarzkopf described as "a horrible, malignant place" called
the Batangan Peninsula. The area had been fought over for
thirty years, was covered with mines and booby traps, and was
the site of numerous weekly casualties from those devices.

Schwarzkopf made the best of a bad situation. He intro-
duced procedures to greatly reduce casualties, and whenever
a soldier *was* injured by a mine, he flew out to check on the

man, had him evacuated using his chopper, and talked to the other soldiers to boost their morale.

On May 28, 1970, a man was injured by a mine, and Schwarzkopf, then a colonel, flew to the man's location. While the helicopter was evacuating the injured soldier, another soldier stepped on a mine, severely injuring his leg. The man thrashed around on the ground, screaming and wailing. That's when everyone realized the first mine hadn't been a lone booby trap. They were all standing in the middle of a minefield.

Schwarzkopf believed the injured man could survive and even keep his leg—but only if he stopped flailing around. There was only one thing he could do. He had to go after the man and immobilize him. Schwarzkopf wrote,

> I started through the minefield, one slow step at a time, staring at the ground, looking for telltale bumps or little prongs sticking up from the dirt. My knees were shaking so hard that each time I took a step, I had to grab my leg and steady it with both hands before I could take another . . . It seemed like a thousand years before I reached the kid.

The 240-pound Schwarzkopf, who had been a wrestler at West Point, then pinned the wounded man and calmed him down. It saved his life. And with the help of an engineer team, Schwarzkopf got him and the others out of the minefield.

The quality that Schwarzkopf displayed that day could be described as heroism, courage, or even foolhardiness. But I think the word that best describes it is *servanthood*. On that day in May, the only way he could be effective as a leader was to serve the soldier who was in trouble.

Having a Servant's Heart

When you think of servanthood, do you envision it as an activity performed by relatively low-skilled people at the bottom of the positional totem pole? If you do, you have a wrong impression. Servanthood is not about position or skill. It's about attitude. You have undoubtedly met people in service positions who have poor attitudes toward servanthood: the rude worker at the government agency, the waiter who can't be bothered with taking your order, the store clerk who talks on the phone with a friend instead of helping you.

Just as you can sense when a worker doesn't want to help people, you can just as easily detect whether someone has a servant's heart. And the truth is that the best leaders desire to serve others, not themselves.

What does it mean to embody the quality of servanthood? A true servant leader:

1. PUTS OTHERS AHEAD OF HIS OWN AGENDA

The first mark of servanthood is the ability to put others ahead of yourself and your personal desires. It is more than being willing to put your agenda on hold. It means intentionally being aware of other people's needs, available to help them, and able to accept their desires as important.

2. POSSESSES THE CONFIDENCE TO SERVE

The real heart of servanthood is security. Show me someone who thinks he is too important to serve, and I'll show you someone who is basically insecure. How we treat others is really a reflection of how we think about ourselves. Philosopher-poet Eric Hoffer captured that thought:

> The remarkable thing is that we really love our neighbor as ourselves; we do unto others as we do unto ourselves. We hate others when we hate ourselves. We are tolerant toward others when we tolerate ourselves. We forgive others when we forgive ourselves. It is not love of self but hatred of self which is at the root of the troubles that afflict our world.

Only secure leaders give power to others. It's also true that only secure people exhibit servanthood.

3. INITIATES SERVICE TO OTHERS

Just about anyone will serve if compelled to do so. And some will serve in a crisis. But you can really see the heart of someone who initiates service to others. Great leaders see the need, seize the opportunity, and serve without expecting anything in return.

4. IS NOT POSITION-CONSCIOUS

Servant leaders don't focus on rank or position. When Colonel Norman Schwarzkopf stepped into that minefield, rank was the last thing on his mind. He was one person trying to help another. If anything, being the leader gave him a greater sense of obligation to serve.

5. SERVES OUT OF LOVE

Servanthood is not motivated by manipulation or self-promotion. It is fueled by love. In the end, the extent of your influence and the quality of your relationships depend on the depth of your concern for others. That's why it's so important for leaders to be willing to serve.

HOW TO BECOME A SERVANT

To improve your servanthood, do the following:

- *Perform small acts.* When was the last time you performed small acts of kindness for others? Start with

those closest to you: your spouse, children, parents.
Find ways today to do small things that show others
you care.

- *Learn to walk slowly through the crowd.* I learned this
  great lesson from my father. I call it walking slowly
  through the crowd. The next time you attend a
  function with a number of clients, colleagues, or
  employees, make it your goal to connect with others
  by circulating among them and talking to people.
  Focus on each person you meet. Learn his name if
  you don't know it already. Make your agenda getting
  to know each person's needs, wants, and desires. Then
  later when you go home, make a note to yourself to
  do something beneficial for half a dozen of those
  people.

IT IS TRUE THAT THOSE WHO WOULD BE GREAT
MUST BE LIKE THE LEAST AND THE SERVANT OF ALL.

- *Move into action.* If an attitude of servanthood is
  conspicuously absent from your life, the best way
  to change it is to start serving. Begin serving with
  your body, and your heart will eventually catch up.
  Sign up to serve others for six months at your church,

a community agency, or a volunteer organization.
If your attitude still isn't good at the end of your
term, do it again. Keep at it until your heart
changes.

Where is your heart when it comes to serving others? Do
you desire to become a leader for the perks and benefits? Or
are you motivated by a desire to help others?

If you really want to become the kind of leader that people
want to follow, you will have to settle the issue of servanthood. If your attitude is to be served rather than to serve, you
may be headed for trouble. It is true that those who would be
great must be like the least and the servant of all.

Albert Schweitzer wisely stated, "I don't know what your
destiny will be, but one thing I know: The ones among you
who will be really happy are those who have sought and
found how to serve." If you want to be successful on the highest level, be willing to serve on the lowest. That's the best way
to build relationships.

NOTES

Chapter 1
1. Michael K. Deaver, "The Ronald Reagan I Knew," *Parade*, 22 April 2001, 12.
2. Ibid., 10.
3. "Thirty Years with Reagan: A Chat with Author, Former Reagan Aide Michael Deaver," 20 April 2001 <www.abc-news.com>.
4. Ibid.

Chapter 2
1. Art Mortell, "How to Master the Inner Game of Selling," vol. 10, no. 7.
2. Ecclesiastes 4:9–12 NIV.

Chapter 3
1. 1 Samuel 17:33–37 NIV.

Chapter 4
1. H. Norman Schwarzkopf, "Lessons in Leadership," vol. 12, no. 5.

2. Kevin and Jackie Freiberg, *Nuts! Southwest Airlines' Crazy Recipe for Business* (New York: Broadway Books, 1996), 224.

Chapter 6

1. Stephen R. Covey, *The Seven Habits of Highly Effective People: Restoring the Character Ethic* (New York: Simon and Schuster, 1989).
2. Proverbs 22:1 NIV.
3. Donald T. Phillips, *Lincoln on Leadership: Executive Strategies for Tough Times* (New York: Warner Books, 1992), 66–67.

Chapter 7

1. Gary Bauer, "American Family Life," *Focus on the Family* magazine, July 1994, 2.
2. William Kirkpatrick, *Why Johnny Can't Tell Right from Wrong* (New York: Simon and Schuster, 1992).
3. Quoted in *Christianity Today*, 4 October 1993.

EQUIPPING

101

WHAT EVERY LEADER NEEDS TO KNOW

JOHN C. MAXWELL

NELSON BUSINESS
A Division of Thomas Nelson Publishers
Since 1798

www.thomasnelson.com

Published in Nashville, Tennessee, by Thomas Nelson, Inc.

Portions of this book have been taken from *Developing the Leaders Around You*, *The 17 Essential Qualities of a Team Player*, and *The 17 Indisputable Laws of Teamwork*.

Library of Congress Cataloging-in-Publication Data

Maxwell, John C., 1947–
Equipping 101 / John C. Maxwell.
p. cm.
Includes bibliographical references.
ISBN 0-7852-6352-7 (hardcover)
1. Teams in the workplace. 2. Leadership. 3. Career development.
4. Mentoring. I. Title.
HD66.M377 2004
658.3'14—dc22
2003021379

Contents

Look at the most successful organizations in the world, and you find not just one leader—you'll see many strong leaders working together to create their success. That doesn't happen by accident. The most successful organizations possess leaders who are equipping others around them, whether that organization is a small business, large corporation, nonprofit, or sports team. When a leader is dedicated to the equipping process, the level of performance within the whole organization rises dramatically.

Fred A. Manske Jr. said, "The greatest leader is willing to train people and develop them to the point that they eventually surpass him or her in knowledge and ability." This volume, by Dr. John C. Maxwell, will help you to unlock the hidden abilities in your people by teaching you to equip them for excellence. "Success for leaders," says Maxwell, "can be defined as the maximum utilization of the abilities of those around them." Maxwell should know. He is someone who has made equipping and developing others the primary focus of his life for over twenty years.

In this concise book, a companion to *Relationships 101, Attitude 101,* and *Leadership 101,* you will be equipped yourself: Not only will you learn why equipping others to lead is the most powerful method for success, but you will also learn how to identify potential leaders, equip them, and then take them to a whole new level once they've been released to lead. It's a process that creates synergy in your organization for the long haul.

PART I

EQUIPPING FOR SUCCESS

I

WHY DO I NEED TO
EQUIP OTHERS?

One is too small a number to achieve greatness.

Who are your personal heroes? Okay, maybe you don't have heroes exactly. Then let me ask you this: Which people do you admire most? Who do you wish you were more like? What people fire you up and get your juices flowing? Do you admire . . .

- Business innovators, such as Sam Walton, Fred Smith, or Bill Gates?

- Great athletes, such as Michael Jordan, Tiger Woods, or Mark McGwire?

- Creative geniuses, such as Pablo Picasso, Buckminster Fuller, or Wolfgang Amadeus Mozart?

- Pop culture icons, such as Marilyn Monroe, Andy Warhol, or Elvis Presley?

- Spiritual leaders, such as John Wesley, Billy Graham, or Mother Teresa?

- Political leaders, such as Alexander the Great, Charlemagne, or Winston Churchill?

- Film industry giants, such as D. W. Griffith, Charlie Chaplin, or Steven Spielberg?

- Architects and engineers, such as Frank Lloyd Wright, the Starrett brothers, or Joseph Strauss?

- Revolutionary thinkers, such as Marie Curie, Thomas Edison, or Albert Einstein?

Or maybe your list includes people in a field I didn't mention.

It's safe to say that we all admire achievers. And we Americans especially love pioneers and bold individualists, people who fight alone, despite the odds or opposition: the settler who carves a place for himself in the wilds of the frontier, the Old West sheriff who resolutely faces an enemy in a gunfight, the pilot who bravely flies solo across the Atlantic Ocean, and the scientist who changes the world through the power of his mind.

THE MYTH OF THE LONE RANGER

As much as we admire solo achievement, the truth is that no lone individual has done anything of value. The belief that one person can do something great is a myth. There are no real Rambos who can take on a hostile army by themselves. Even the Lone Ranger wasn't really a loner. Everywhere he went he rode with Tonto!

Nothing of significance was ever achieved by an individual acting alone. Look below the surface and you will find that all seemingly solo acts are really team efforts. Frontiersman Daniel Boone had companions from the Transylvania Company as he blazed the Wilderness Road. Sheriff Wyatt Earp had his two brothers and Doc Holliday looking out for him. Aviator Charles Lindbergh had the backing of nine businessmen from St. Louis and the services of the Ryan Aeronautical Company, which built his plane. Even Albert Einstein, the scientist who revolutionized the world with his theory of relativity, didn't work in a vacuum. Of the debt he owed to others for his work, Einstein once remarked, "Many times a day I realize how much my own outer and inner life is built upon the labors of my fellow men, both living and dead, and how earnestly I must exert myself in order to give in return as much as I have received." It's true that the history of our country is marked by the accomplishments of many

strong leaders and innovative individuals who took consider-
able risks. But those people always were part of teams.

Economist Lester C. Thurow commented on the subject:

> There is nothing antithetical in American history, culture,
> or traditions to teamwork. Teams were important in
> America's history—wagon trains conquered the West, men
> working together on the assembly line in American indus-
> try conquered the world, a successful national strategy and
> a lot of teamwork put an American on the moon first (and
> thus far, last). But American mythology extols only the
> individual . . . In America, halls of fame exist for almost
> every conceivable activity, but nowhere do Americans raise
> monuments in praise of teamwork.

I must say that I don't agree with all of Thurow's conclusions.
After all, I've seen the U.S. Marine Corps war memorial in
Washington, D.C., commemorating the raising of the flag
on Iwo Jima. But he is right about something. Teamwork is
and always has been essential to building this country. And
that statement can be made about every country around the
world.

A Chinese proverb states, "Behind an able man there are
always other able men." And the truth is that teamwork is at
the heart of great achievement. The question isn't whether

teams have value. The question is whether we acknowledge that fact and become better team players. That's why I assert that one is too small a number to achieve greatness. You cannot do anything of real value alone. If you truly take this to heart, you will begin to see the value of developing and equipping your team players.

"BEHIND AN ABLE MAN THERE ARE ALWAYS
OTHER ABLE MEN."—CHINESE PROVERB

I challenge you to think of one act of genuine significance in the history of humankind that was performed by a lone human being. No matter what you name, you will find that a team of people was involved. That is why President Lyndon Johnson said, "There are no problems we cannot solve together, and very few that we can solve by ourselves."

C. Gene Wilkes, in his book, *Jesus on Leadership,* observed that the power of teams not only is evident in today's modern business world, but it also has a deep history that is evident even in biblical times. Wilkes asserts:

- Teams involve more people, thus affording more resources, ideas, and energy than would an individual.

- Teams maximize a leader's potential and minimize her weaknesses. Strengths and weaknesses are more exposed in individuals.

- Teams provide multiple perspectives on how to meet a need or reach a goal, thus devising several alternatives for each situation.

- Teams share the credit for victories and the blame for losses. This fosters genuine humility and authentic community.

- Teams keep leaders accountable for the goal.

- Teams can simply do more than an individual.

If you want to reach your potential or strive for the seemingly impossible—such as communicating your message two thousand years after you are gone—you need to become a team player. It may be a cliché, but it is nonetheless true: Individuals play the game, but teams win championships.

WHY DO WE STAND ALONE?

Knowing all that we do about the potential of teams, why do some people still want to do things by themselves? I believe there are a number of reasons.

1. EGO

Few people are fond of admitting that they can't do everything, yet that is a reality of life. There are no supermen or superwomen. So the question is not whether you can do everything by yourself; it's how soon you're going to realize that you can't.

Philanthropist Andrew Carnegie declared, "It marks a big step in your development when you come to realize that other people can help you do a better job than you could do alone." To do something really big, let go of your ego, and get ready to be part of a team.

2. INSECURITY

In my work with leaders, I've found that some individuals fail to promote teamwork and fail to equip their team members for leadership because they feel threatened by other people. Sixteenth-century Florentine statesman Niccolò Machiavelli probably made similar observations, prompting him to write, "The first method for estimating the intelligence of a ruler is to look at the men he has around him."

I believe that insecurity, rather than poor judgment or lack of intelligence, most often causes leaders to surround themselves with weak people. Only secure leaders give power to others. On the other hand, insecure leaders usually fail to build teams because of one of two reasons: Either they want to maintain control over everything for which they are responsible, or they fear being replaced by someone more capable. In either case, leaders who fail to promote teamwork undermine their own potential and erode the best efforts of the people with whom they work. They would benefit from the advice of President Woodrow Wilson: "We should not only use all the brains we have, but all that we can borrow."

"THE FIRST METHOD FOR ESTIMATING THE INTELLIGENCE OF A RULER IS TO LOOK AT THE MEN HE HAS AROUND HIM."—NICCOLÒ MACHIAVELLI

---

3. NAIVETÉ

Consultant John Ghegan keeps a sign on his desk that says, "If I had it to do all over again, I'd get help." That remark accurately represents the feelings of the third type of people who fail to become team builders. They naively underestimate the difficulty of achieving big things. As a result, they try to go it alone.

Some people who start out in this group turn out okay in the end. They discover that their dreams are bigger than their capabilities, they realize they won't accomplish their goals solo, and they adjust. They make team building their approach to achievement. But some others learn the truth too late, and as a result, they never accomplish their goals. And that's a shame.

4. TEMPERAMENT

Some people aren't very outgoing and simply don't think in terms of team building and equipping. As they face challenges, it never occurs to them to enlist others to achieve something.

As a people person, I find that hard to relate to. Whenever I face any kind of challenge, the very first thing I do is to think about the people I want on the team to help with it. I've been that way since I was a kid. I've always thought, *Why take the journey alone when you can invite others along with you?*

I understand that not everyone operates that way. But whether or not you are naturally inclined to be part of a team is really irrelevant. If you do everything alone and never partner with other people, you create huge barriers to your own potential. Dr. Allan Fromme quipped, "People have been known to achieve more as a result of working with others than against them." What an understatement! It takes a team to do anything of lasting value. Besides, even the most introverted person in the world can learn to enjoy the benefits of being on a team. (That's true even if someone isn't trying to accomplish something great.)

A few years ago my friend Chuck Swindoll wrote a piece in *The Finishing Touch* that sums up the importance of teamwork. He said,

Nobody is a whole team . . . We need each other. You need someone and someone needs you. Isolated islands we're not. To make this thing called life work, we gotta lean and support. And relate and respond. And give and take. And confess and forgive. And reach out and embrace and rely . . . Since none of us is a whole, independent, self-sufficient, super-capable, all-powerful hotshot, let's quit acting like we are. Life's lonely enough without our playing that silly role. The game is over. Let's link up.

For the person trying to do everything alone, the game really is over. If you want to do something big, you must link up with others. One is too small a number to achieve greatness.

HOW CAN I ADOPT A TEAM MIND-SET?

Investing in a team almost guarantees a high return for the effort, because a team can do so much more than individuals.

He's one of the greatest team builders in all of sports, yet you've probably never heard of him. Here is a list of his impressive accomplishments:

- Forty consecutive basketball seasons with at least twenty wins

- Five national championships

- Number one ranking in his region in twenty of the last thirty-three years

- Lifetime winning percentage of .870

His name is Morgan Wootten. And why have most people never heard of him? Because he is a high school basketball coach!

When asked to name the greatest basketball coach of all time, most people would respond with one of two names: Red Auerbach or John Wooden. But do you know what John Wooden, the UCLA coach called the Wizard of Westwood, had to say about Morgan Wootten? He was emphatic in his appraisal: "People say Morgan Wootten is the best high school coach in the country. I disagree. I know of no finer coach at any level—high school, college or pro. I've said it elsewhere and I'll say it here: I stand in awe of him."[1]

That's a pretty strong recommendation from the man who won ten NCAA national championships and coached some of the most talented players in the game, including Kareem Abdul-Jabbar. (By the way, when Kareem was in high school at Power Memorial Academy, his team lost only one game—to Morgan Wootten's team!)

NO PLAN TO BE A TEAM BUILDER

Morgan Wootten never planned to coach a team. He was a decent athlete in high school, but nothing special. However, he was an excellent talker. When he was growing up, his ambition was to be an attorney. But when he was a nineteen-year-old college student, a friend tricked him into accepting a job coaching baseball, a game he knew little about, to kids from an orphanage. The team had no uniforms and no equipment. And despite working hard, the boys lost all sixteen of their games.

During that first season, Wootten fell in love with those kids. When they asked him to come back and coach football, he couldn't refuse them. Besides, he had played football in high school, so he knew something about it. The orphanage team went undefeated and won the Washington, D.C., Catholic Youth Organization (CYO) championship. But more important, Wootten began to realize that he wanted to invest his time in children, not in court cases.

Even that first year he made a difference in the lives of kids. He remembers one boy in particular who had started stealing and kept being brought back to the orphanage by the police. He described the boy as having "two and a half strikes against him already." Wootten let the boy know he was headed for trouble. But he also took the boy under his wing. Wootten recalled,

We started spending some time together. I took him to my house and he'd enjoy Mom's meals. He spent weekends with us. He became friends with my brother and sisters. He's still in Washington today and doing quite well and known to a lot of people. Anyone would be proud to call him their son. He was bound for a life of crime and jail, however, and maybe a lot worse, until someone gave him the greatest gift a parent can give a child—his time.

Giving of himself to the people on his teams is something Wootten has done every year since then. NCAA basketball coach Marty Fletcher, a former player and assistant under Wootten, summarized his talent this way: "His secret is that he makes whomever he is with feel like the most important person in the world."[2]

Creating a Dynasty

It wasn't long before Wootten was invited to become an assistant coach at a local powerhouse high school. Then with a couple of years' experience under his belt, he became head coach at DeMatha High School.

When he started at the school in 1956, Wootten was taking over a bunch of losing teams. He called together all of the students who wanted to play sports at DeMatha, and he told them:

Fellas, things are going to change. I know how bad DeMatha's teams have been during these last few years, but that's over with. We're going to win at DeMatha and we're going to build a tradition of winning. Starting right now . . . But let me tell you how we're going to do it. We're going to outwork every team we ever play . . . With a lot of hard work and discipline and dedication, people are going to hear about us and respect us, because DeMatha will be a winner.[3]

That year, the football team won half of its games, which was quite an accomplishment. In basketball and baseball, they were division champions. His teams have been winning ever since. DeMatha has long been considered a dynasty.

On October 13, 2000, Wootten was inducted into the Naismith Basketball Hall of Fame in Springfield, Massachusetts. At that time, his teams had amassed a record of 1,210-183. Over the years, more than 250 of his players have won college scholarships. Twelve players from his high school teams went on to play in the NBA.[4]

It's Not About Basketball

But winning games and honors isn't what excites Wootten most. It's investing in the kids. Wootten says,

Coaches at every level have a tendency to lose sight of their purpose at times, especially after success arrives. They

start to put the cart before the horse by working harder
and harder to develop their teams, using their boys or girls
to do it, gradually forgetting that their real purpose should
be to develop the kids, using their teams to do it.[5]

Wootten's attitude reaps rewards not only for the team, but
also for the individuals on the team. For example, for a
twenty-six-year stretch, every single one of Wootten's seniors
earned college scholarships—not just starters but bench players too.

Equipping your team compounds over time. Morgan
Wootten equips his players because it is the right thing to
do, because he cares about them. That practice has made
his players good, his teams successful, and his career
remarkable. He is the first basketball coach to have won
1,200 games at any level. Developing people pays off in
every way.

HOW TO INVEST IN YOUR TEAM

I believe that most people recognize that investing in a team
brings benefits to everyone on the team. The question for
most people isn't why, but how. Allow me to share with you
ten steps you can take to invest in your team.

Here is how to get started:

1. Make the Decision to Build a Team—This Starts the Investment in the Team

It's said that every journey begins with the first step. Deciding that people on the team are worth equipping and developing is the first step in building a better team. That requires commitment.

2. Gather the Best Team Possible—This Elevates the Potential of the Team

The better the people on the team, the greater the potential. There's only one kind of team that you may be a part of where you shouldn't go out and find the best players available, and that's family. You need to stick with those teammates through thick and thin. But every other kind of team can benefit from the recruitment of the very best people available.

3. Pay the Price to Develop the Team—This Ensures the Growth of the Team

When Morgan Wootten extended himself to benefit the kid who had two-and-a-half strikes against him, he and his family had to pay a price to help that boy. It wasn't convenient or comfortable. It cost them in energy, money, and time.

It will cost you to develop your team. You will have to dedicate time that could be used for personal productivity. You will have to spend money that could be used for personal benefit. And sometimes you will have to set aside your personal agenda.

4. DO THINGS TOGETHER AS A TEAM—THIS PROVIDES COMMUNITY FOR THE TEAM

I once read the statement, "Even when you've played the game of your life, it's the feeling of teamwork that you'll remember. You'll forget the plays, the shots, and the scores, but you'll never forget your teammates." That is describing the community that develops among teammates who spend time doing things together.

DECIDING THAT PEOPLE ON THE TEAM ARE WORTH EQUIPPING AND DEVELOPING IS THE FIRST STEP IN BUILDING A BETTER TEAM.

The only way to develop community and cohesiveness among your teammates is to get them together, not just in a professional setting but in personal ones as well. There are lots of ways to get yourself connected with your teammates, and to connect them with one another. Many families who want to bond find that camping does the trick. Business colleagues can socialize outside work (in an appropriate way). The where and when are not as important as the fact that team members share common experiences.

5. Empower Team Members with Responsibility and Authority—This Raises Up Leaders for the Team

The greatest growth for people often occurs as a result of the trial and error of personal experience. Any team that wants people to step up to a higher level of performance—and to higher levels of leadership—must give team members authority as well as responsibility. If you are a leader on your team, don't protect your position or hoard your power. Give it away. That's the only way to empower your team.

6. Give Credit for Success to the Team—This Lifts the Morale of the Team

Mark Twain said, "I can live for two months on one good compliment." That's the way most people feel. They are willing to work hard if they receive recognition for their efforts. Compliment your teammates. Talk up their accomplishments. And if you're the leader, take the blame but never the credit. Do that and your team will always fight for you.

"I can live for two months on one good compliment."—Mark Twain

---

7. Watch to See That the Investment in the Team Is Paying Off—This Brings Accountability to the Team

If you put money into an investment, you expect a return—maybe not right away, but certainly over time. How will you know whether you are gaining or losing ground on that investment? You have to pay attention to it and measure its progress.

The same is true of an investment in people. You need to observe whether you are getting a return for the time, energy, and resources you are putting into them. Some people develop quickly. Others are slower to respond, and that's okay. The main outcome you want to see is progress.

8. Stop Your Investment in Players Who Do Not Grow—This Eliminates Greater Losses for the Team

One of the most difficult experiences for any team member is leaving a teammate behind. Yet that is what you must do if someone on your team refuses to grow or change for the benefit of teammates. That doesn't mean that you love the person less. It just means you stop spending your time trying to invest in someone who won't or can't make the team better.

9. Create New Opportunities for the Team—This Allows the Team to Stretch

There is no greater investment you can make in a team than giving it new opportunities. When a team has the possibility of taking new ground or facing new challenges, it has to stretch to meet them. That process not only gives the team a chance to grow, but it also benefits every individual. Everyone has the opportunity to grow toward his or her potential.

10. Give the Team the Best Possible Chance to Succeed—This Guarantees the Team a High Return

James E. Hunton says, "Coming together is a beginning. Keeping together is progress. Working together is success." One of the most essential tasks you can undertake is to clear obstacles so that the team has the best possible chance to work toward success. If you are a team member, that may mean making a personal sacrifice or helping others to work together better. If you are a leader, that means creating an energized environment for the team and equipping each person with what he needs at any given time to ensure success.

Investing in a team almost guarantees a high return for the effort, because a team can do so much more than individuals. Or as Rex Murphy, one of my conference attendees, told me: "Where there's a will there's a way; where there's a team, there's more than one way."

My Personal Investment—and Return

Once you have experienced what it means to invest in your team, you will never be able to stop. Thinking about my team—about how the teammates add value to me as I add value to them—brings me abundant joy. And just like my investment and their return, my joy continues to compound.

At this stage of my life, everything I do is a team effort. When I first started teaching seminars, I did everything. Certainly there were other people pitching in, but I was just as likely to pack and ship a box as I was to speak. Now, I show up and teach. My wonderful team takes care of everything else. Even the book you're reading was a team effort. I would do anything for the people on my team because they do everything for me:

My team makes me better than I am.
My team multiplies my value to others.
My team enables me to do what I do best.
My team gives me more time.
My team represents me where I cannot go.
My team provides community for our enjoyment.
My team fulfills the desires of my heart.

If your current team experiences are not as positive as you would like, then it's time to increase your level of investment. Building and equipping a team for the future is just like developing a financial nest egg. It may start slowly, but what you put in brings a high return—similar to the way that compound interest works with finances. Try it and you will find that investing in the team compounds over time.

PART II

EQUIPPING THE RIGHT PEOPLE

3

———

Whom Should
I Equip?

*Those closest to the leader will determine the
success level of that leader.*

One night, after working quite late, I grabbed a copy of *Sports Illustrated*, hoping its pages would lull me to sleep. It had the opposite effect. On the back cover was an advertisement that caught my eye and got my emotional juices flowing. It featured a picture of John Wooden, the coach who led the UCLA Bruins for many years. The caption beneath his picture read, "The guy who puts the ball through the hoop has ten hands."

John Wooden was a great basketball coach. Called the Wizard of Westwood, he brought ten national basketball championships to UCLA in a span of twelve years. Two back-to-back championships are almost unheard of in the world of competitive sports, but he led the Bruins to *seven titles in a row.* It took a consistent level of superior play, good coaching, and hard practice. But the key to the Bruins's success was

Coach Wooden's unyielding dedication to his concept of teamwork.

He knew that if you oversee people and you wish to develop leaders, you are responsible to: (1) appreciate them for who they are; (2) believe that they will do their very best; (3) praise their accomplishments; and (4) accept your personal responsibility to them as their leader.

Coach Bear Bryant expressed this same sentiment when he said: "I'm just a plowhand from Arkansas, but I have learned how to hold a team together—how to lift some men up, how to calm others down, until finally they've got one heartbeat together as a team. There's always just three things I say: 'If anything goes bad, I did it. If anything goes semi-good, then we did it. If anything goes real good, they did it.' That's all it takes to get people to win." Bear Bryant won people and games. Until a few years ago, he held the title of the winningest coach in the history of college football, with 323 victories.

Great leaders—the truly successful ones who are in the top 1 percent—all have one thing in common. They know that acquiring and keeping good people is a leader's most important task. An organization cannot increase its productivity—but people can! The asset that truly appreciates within any organization is people. Systems become dated. Buildings deteriorate. Machinery wears. But people can grow, develop, and become more effective if they have a leader who understands their potential value.

If you really want to be a successful leader, you must develop and equip other leaders around you. You must find a way to get your vision seen, implemented, and contributed to by your team. The leader sees the big picture, but he needs other leaders to help make his mental picture a reality.

Most leaders have followers around them. They believe the key to leadership is gaining more *followers*. Few leaders surround themselves with other *leaders,* but the ones who do bring great value to their organizations. And not only is their burden lightened, but their vision is carried on and enlarged.

WHOM YOU EQUIP REALLY MATTERS

The key to surrounding yourself with other leaders is to find the best people you can, then equip them to become the best leaders they can be. Great leaders produce other leaders. Let me tell you why:

THOSE CLOSEST TO THE LEADER WILL DETERMINE THE SUCCESS LEVEL OF THAT LEADER

The greatest leadership principle that I have learned in over thirty years of leadership is that those closest to the leader will determine the success level of that leader. A negative reading of this statement is also true: Those closest to the leader will determine the level of failure for that leader. In other words, the people close to me "make me or break me." The determination of a positive or negative outcome in my leadership depends upon my ability as a leader to develop and equip those closest to me. It also depends upon my ability to recognize the value that others bring to my organization. My goal is not to draw a following that results in a crowd. My goal is to develop leaders who become a movement.

Stop for a moment and think of the five or six people closest to you in your organization. Are you developing them? Do you have a game plan for their growth? Are they being properly equipped for leadership? Have they been able to lift your load?

Within my organization leadership development is continually emphasized. In their first training session, I give new leaders this principle: *As a potential leader you are either an asset or a liability to the organization.* I illustrate this truth by saying, "When there's a problem, a 'fire' in the organization, you as a leader are often the first to arrive at the scene. You have in your hands two buckets. One contains water and the other contains gasoline. The 'spark' before you will either become a greater problem because you pour the gasoline on it, or it will be extinguished because you use the bucket of water."

Every person within your organization also carries two

buckets. The question a leader needs to ask is, "Am I training them to use the gasoline or the water?"

An Organization's Growth Potential Is Directly Related to Its Personnel Potential

When conducting leadership conferences, I often make the statement, "Grow a leader—grow the organization." A company cannot grow without until its leaders grow within.

I am often amazed at the amount of money, energy, and marketing focus organizations spend on areas that will not produce growth. Why advertise that the customer is number one when the personnel have not been trained in customer service? When customers arrive, they will know the difference between an employee who has been trained to give service and one who hasn't. Slick brochures and catchy slogans will never overcome incompetent leadership.

In 1981 I became Senior Pastor of Skyline Wesleyan Church in San Diego, California. This congregation had averaged 1,000 in attendance from 1969 to 1981, and it was obviously on a plateau. When I assumed leadership responsibilities, the first question I asked was, "Why has the growth stopped?" I needed to find an answer, so I called my first staff meeting and gave a lecture titled *The Leadership Line*. My thesis was, "Leaders determine the level of an organization." I drew a line across a marker board and wrote the number

1,000. I shared with the staff that for thirteen years the average attendance at Skyline was 1,000. I knew the staff could lead 1,000 people effectively. What I did not know was whether they could lead 2,000 people. So I drew a dotted line and wrote the number 2,000, and I placed a question mark between the two lines. I then drew an arrow from the bottom 1,000 to the top 2,000 line and wrote the word "change."

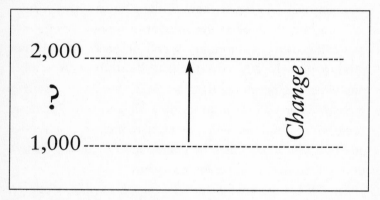

It would be my responsibility to equip them and help them make the necessary changes to reach our new goal. When the leaders changed positively, I knew the growth would come automatically. Now, I had to help them change themselves, or I knew I would literally have to change them by hiring others to take their places.

From 1981 to 1995 I gave this lecture at Skyline on three occasions. The last time, the number 4,000 was placed on the top line. As I discovered, the numbers changed, but the lecture didn't. The strength of any organization is a direct result of the strength of its leaders. Weak leaders equal weak organizations. Strong leaders equal strong organizations. Everything rises and falls on leadership.

POTENTIAL LEADERS HELP CARRY THE LOAD

Businessman Rolland Young said, "I am a self-made man, but I think if I had it to do over again, I would call in someone else!" Usually leaders fail to develop other leaders either because they lack training or because they possess wrong attitudes about allowing and encouraging others to come alongside them. Often, leaders wrongly believe that they must compete with the people close to them instead of working with them. Great leaders have a different mind-set. In *Profiles in Courage*, President John F. Kennedy wrote, "The best way to go along is to get along with others." This kind of positive interaction can happen only if the leader has an attitude of interdependency with others and is committed to win-win relationships.

EVERYTHING RISES AND FALLS ON LEADERSHIP.

Take a look at differences between the two views leaders possess about people:

WINNING BY COMPETITIVENESS	WINNING BY COOPERATION
Look at others as enemies	Look at others as friends
Concentrate on yourself	Concentrate on others
Become suspicious of others	Become supportive of others
Win only if you are good	Win if you or others are good
Winning determined by your skills	Winning determined by the skills of many
Small victory	Large victory
Some joy	Much joy
There are winners and losers	There are only winners

Peter Drucker was correct when he said, "No executive has ever suffered because his people were strong and effective." The leaders around me lift my load in many ways. Here are two of the most important ones:

1. *They become a sounding board for me.* As a leader, I sometimes hear counsel that I don't want to hear but need to hear. That's the advantage of having leaders around you—having people who know how to make decisions. Followers tell you what you *want* to hear. Leaders tell you what you *need* to hear.

I have always encouraged those closest to me to give me advice on the front end. In other words, an opinion before a decision has potential value. An opinion after the decision has been made is worthless. Alex Agase, a college football coach, once said, "If you really want to give me advice, do it on Saturday afternoon between one and four o'clock, when you've got twenty-five seconds to do it, between plays. Don't give me advice on Monday. I know the right thing to do on Monday."

"NO EXECUTIVE HAS EVER SUFFERED BECAUSE HIS PEOPLE WERE STRONG AND EFFECTIVE."—PETER DRUCKER

---

2. They possess a leadership mind-set. Fellow leaders do more than work with the leader, they think like the leader. It gives them the power to lighten the load. This becomes invaluable in areas such as decision making, brainstorming, and providing security and direction to others.

A majority of my time is spent away from the office speaking at conferences and events. Therefore, it is essential that I have leaders in my organizations who can carry on effectively while I am gone. And they do. It happens because I have spent my life finding and developing potential leaders. The results are very gratifying.

LEADERS ATTRACT POTENTIAL LEADERS

Birds of a feather really do flock together. I really believe that it takes a leader to know a leader, grow a leader, and show a leader. I have also found that it takes a leader to attract a leader.

Attraction is the obvious first step to equipping others, yet I find many people in leadership positions who are unable to accomplish this task. Good leaders are able to attract potential leaders because:

- Leaders think like them.

- Leaders express feelings that other leaders sense.

- Leaders create an environment that attracts potential leaders.

- Leaders are not threatened by people with great potential.

For example, a person in a leadership position who is a "5" on a scale of 1 to 10 will not attract a leader who is a "9." Why? Because leaders naturally size up any crowd and migrate to other leaders who are at the same or higher level.

Any leader who has only followers around him will be called upon to continually draw on his own resources to get things done. Without other leaders to carry the load, he will become fatigued and burnt out. Have you asked yourself lately, "Am I tired?" If the answer is yes, you may have a good reason for it, as this humorous story illustrates:

Somewhere in the world there is a country with a population of 220 million. Eighty-four million are over sixty years of age, which leaves 136 million to do the work. People under twenty years of age total 95 million, which leaves 41 million to do the work.

There are 22 million employed by the government, which leaves 19 million to do the work. Four million are in the Armed Forces, which leaves 15 million to do the work. Deduct 14,800,000, the number in state and city offices, and that leaves 200,000 to do the work. There are 188,000 in hospitals or insane asylums, so that leaves 12,000 to do the work.

It is of interest to note that in this country 11,998 people are in jail, so that leaves just two people to carry the load. That's you and me—and brother, I'm getting tired of doing everything myself!

Unless you want to carry the whole load yourself, you need to be developing and equipping leaders.

Equipped Leaders Expand and Enhance the Future of the Organization

One of the things my father taught me was the importance of people above all other elements in an organization. He was the president of a college for sixteen years. One day, as we sat on a campus bench, he explained that the most expensive workers on campus were not the highest paid. The most expensive ones were the people who were nonproductive. He explained that developing leaders took time and cost money. You usually had to pay leaders more. But such people were an invaluable asset. They attracted a higher quality of person; they were more productive; and they continued to add value to the organization. He closed the conversation by saying, "Most people produce only when they feel like it. Leaders produce even when they don't feel like it."

"Most people produce only when they feel like it. Leaders produce even when they don't feel like it."—Melvin Maxwell

---

The More People You Lead, the More Leaders You Need

Zig Ziglar says, "Success is the maximum utilization of the ability that you have." I believe a leader's success can be defined as *the maximum utilization of the abilities of those under him.* Andrew Carnegie explained it like this: "I wish to have as my epitaph: 'Here lies a man who was wise enough to bring into his service men who knew more than he.'" That is a worthy goal for any leader.

4

WHAT DOES A POTENTIAL LEADER LOOK LIKE?

Great leaders seek out and find potential leaders,
then transform them into good leaders.

There is something much more important and scarce than ability: It is the ability to recognize ability. One of the primary responsibilities of a successful leader is to identify potential leaders. These are the people in whom you will want to invest your time equipping. Identifying them is not always an easy job, but it is critical.

Andrew Carnegie was a master at identifying potential leaders. Once asked by a reporter how he had managed to hire forty-three millionaires, Carnegie responded that the men had not been millionaires when they started working for him. They had become millionaires as a result. The reporter next wanted to know how he had developed these men to become such valuable leaders. Carnegie replied, "Men are developed the same way gold is mined. Several tons of dirt must be moved to get an ounce of gold. But you don't go into the mine looking for dirt," he added. "You go in looking for the gold." That's exactly the way to develop positive, successful people. Look for the gold, not the dirt; the good, not the bad. The more positive qualities you look for, the more you are going to find.

Selecting the Right Players

Professional sports organizations recognize the importance of selecting the right players. Every year, coaches and owners of professional baseball, basketball, and football teams look forward to the draft. To prepare for it, sports franchises spend much time and energy scouting new prospects. For instance, scouts from pro football organizations travel to regular-season college games, bowl games, senior-only bowl games, and camps to gain knowledge about prospective players. All of this enables the scouts to bring plenty of information back to the owners and head coaches so that when draft day arrives, the teams can pick the most promising players. Team owners and coaches know that the future success of their teams depends largely on their ability to draft effectively.

It's no different in business. You must select the right players in your organization. If you select well, the benefits are multiplied and seem nearly endless. If you select poorly, the problems are multiplied and seem endless.

The key to making the right choice depends on two things:

(1) your ability to see the big picture, and (2) your ability to judge potential employees during the selection process.

It is a good idea to start with an inventory. I use this one because I always want to look inside as well as outside the organization to find candidates. I call this list the Five A's:

Assessment of needs:	What is needed?
Assets on hand:	Who in the organization is available?
Ability of candidates:	Who is able?
Attitude of candidates:	Who is willing?
Accomplishments of candidates:	Who gets things done?

Notice that the inventory begins with an assessment of needs. The leader of the organization must base that assessment on the big picture. While he was manager of the Chicago Cubs, Charlie Grimm reportedly received a phone call from one of his scouts. The man was excited and began to shout over the telephone, "Charlie, I've landed the greatest young pitcher in the land! He struck out every man who came to bat. Twenty-seven in a row. Nobody even hit a foul until the ninth inning. The pitcher is right here with me. What shall I do?" Charlie replied, "Sign up the guy who got the foul. We're looking for hitters." Charlie knew what the team needed.

There is one situation that supersedes a needs analysis:

When a truly exceptional person is available but doesn't necessarily match the current need, do whatever you can to hire him or her anyway. In the long run, that person will positively impact the organization. You see this kind of decision making in sports. Football coaches generally draft players to fill specific needs. If they lack a strong running back, they draft the best running back available. But sometimes they get an opportunity to draft an "impact player," a superstar who can instantly change the whole complexion of the team. Incidentally, impact players usually possess not only athletic ability but also leadership skills. Even as rookies, they have all the qualities to be team captains. When I have an opportunity to hire someone who is exceptional—a superstar—I do it. Then I find a place for him or her. Good people are hard to find, and there is always room for one more productive person in an organization.

QUALITIES TO LOOK FOR IN A LEADER

To find leaders to equip, you first need to know what they look like. Here are ten leadership qualities to seek in anyone you hire:

1. CHARACTER

The first thing to look for in any kind of leader or potential leader is strength of character. I have found nothing more important than this quality. Serious character flaws cannot be ignored. They will eventually make a leader ineffective— every time.

Character flaws should not be confused with weaknesses. We all have weaknesses. They can be overcome through training or experience. Character flaws cannot be changed overnight. Change usually takes a long period of time and involves significant relational investment and dedication on the part of the leader. Any person that you hire who has character flaws will be the weak link in your organization. Depending on the nature of the character flaw, the person has the potential to destroy the organization.

Some of the qualities that make up good character include: honesty, integrity, self-discipline, teachability, dependability, perseverance, conscientiousness, and a strong work ethic. The words of a person with right character match the deeds. His reputation is solid. His manner is straightforward.

The assessment of character can be difficult. Warning signs to watch for include:

- A person's failure to take responsibility for his actions or circumstances

- Unfulfilled promises or obligations

- Failure to meet deadlines

You can tell much about a person's ability to lead others from how well he manages his own life. Look at his interaction with others too. You can tell much about a person's character from his relationships. Examine his relationships with superiors, colleagues, and subordinates. Talk to your employees to find out how the potential leader treats them. This will give you additional insight.

LEADERSHIP IS INFLUENCE.

---

2. INFLUENCE

Leadership is influence. Every leader has these two characteristics: (A) he is going somewhere; and (B) he is able to persuade others to go with him. Influence by itself is not enough. That influence must be measured to determine its *quality*. When looking at a potential leader's influence, examine the following:

What is the leader's level of influence? Does that person have followers due to position (he uses the power of his job title), permission (he has developed relationships which motivate), production (he and his followers consistently produce results), personnel development (he has developed others around him), or personhood (he transcends the organization and develops people on a world-class scale)?

Who influences the leader? Who is she following? People become like their models. Is her model ethical? Does her model have the right priorities?

Whom does he influence? Likewise, the quality of the follower will indicate the quality of the leader. Are his followers positive producers or a bunch of mediocre yes-men?

Stuart Briscoe, in *Discipleship for Ordinary People*, tells the story of a young clergyman who officiated at the funeral of a war veteran. The veteran's military friends wanted to participate in the service to honor their comrade, so they requested that the young pastor lead them down to the casket for a moment of remembrance and then out through a side door. The occasion failed to have the desired effect when the clergyman led them through the wrong door. In full view of the other mourners, the men marched with military precision into a broom closet and had to beat a hasty and confused retreat. Every leader must know where he is going. And every follower had better be sure he's behind a leader who knows what he's doing.

3. POSITIVE ATTITUDE

A positive attitude is one of the most valuable assets a person can have in life. My belief in this is so strong that I wrote an entire book on the subject, *The Winning Attitude: Your Key to Personal Success*. So often, what people say their problem is really isn't their problem. Their problem is the attitude that causes them to handle life's obstacles poorly.

The individual whose attitude causes him to approach life from an entirely positive perspective is someone who can be called a no-limit person. In other words, the person doesn't accept the normal limitations of life as most people do. He is determined to walk to the very edge of his potential, or his product's potential, before he accepts defeat. People with positive attitudes are able to go places where others can't. They do things that others can't. They are not restricted by self-imposed limitations.

A person with a positive attitude is like a bumblebee. The bumblebee should not be able to fly, because the size, weight, and shape of its body in relationship to its wingspread makes flying aerodynamically impossible. But the bumblebee, being ignorant of scientific theory, flies anyway and makes honey every day.

This no-limit mind-set allows a person to start each day with a positive disposition, as did an elevator operator I once read about. One Monday morning, in a full elevator, the man began humming a tune. One passenger, irritated by the man's mood, snapped, "What are you so happy about?" "Well, sir," replied the operator happily, "I ain't never lived this day before." Not only does the future look bright when the attitude is right, but the present is much more enjoyable too. The positive person understands that the journey is as enjoyable as the destination.

Think of the attitude like this:

> It is the advance man of our true selves.
> Its roots are inward but its fruit is outward.
> It is our best friend or our worst enemy.
> It is more honest and more consistent than our words.
> It is an outward look based on past experiences.
> It is a thing which draws people to us or repels them.
> It is never content until it is expressed.
> It is the librarian of our past.
> It is the speaker of our present.
> It is the prophet of our future.[1]

Attitude sets the tone, not only for the leader with the attitude, but for the people following him or her.

4. Excellent People Skills

A leader without people skills soon has no followers. Andrew Carnegie, a fantastic leader, is reported to have paid Charles Schwab a salary of $1 million a year simply because of his excellent people skills. Carnegie had other leaders who understood the job better and whose experience and training were better suited to the work. But they lacked the essential human quality of being able to get others to help them, and Schwab could get the best out of his fellow workers. People may admire a person who has only talent and ability, but they will not follow him—not for long.

Excellent people skills involve a genuine concern for others, the ability to understand people, and the decision to make positive interaction with others a primary concern. Our behavior toward others determines their behavior toward us. A successful leader knows this.

5. Evident Gifts

Every person God creates has gifts. One of our jobs as leaders is to make an assessment of those gifts when considering a person for employment or for equipping. I think of every job candidate as a "wanna be" leader. My observation is that there are four types of wanna-bes:

Never be. Some people simply lack the ability to do a particular job. They simply are not gifted for the particular task at hand. A *never be* who is directed into an area where he is not gifted becomes frustrated, often blames others for his lack of success, and eventually burns out. Redirected, he has a chance of reaching his potential.

Could be. A *could be* is a person with the right gifts and abilities but lacking self-discipline. She may even be a person with superstar abilities who just can't get herself to perform. This person needs to develop the self-discipline to "just do it."

Should be. A *should be* is someone with raw talent (gifts) but few skills for harnessing that ability. He needs training. Once he is given help in developing those skills, he will begin to become the person he was created to be.

Must be. The only thing a *must be* lacks is opportunity. She has the right gifts, the right skills, and the right attitude. She has the drive to be the person she was created to be. It is up to you to be the leader who gives her that opportunity. If you don't, she will find someone else who will.

God creates all people with natural gifts. But He also makes them with two ends, one to sit on and one to think with. Success in life is dependent on which one of these ends is used the most, and it's a toss-up: Heads you win, and tails you lose!

6. Proven Track Record

Poet Archibald MacLeish once said, "There is only one thing more painful than learning from experience, and that is not learning from experience." Leaders who learn this truth develop successful track records over time. Everyone who breaks new ground, who strives to do something, makes mistakes. People without proven track records either haven't learned from their mistakes or haven't tried.

I've worked with many talented people who've established tremendous track records. When I first started my organization, one man stood out as a first-rate leader capable of the highest quality of leadership: Dick Peterson. He had worked with IBM for years, and he quickly demonstrated that experience had not been wasted on him. Dick already had a proven track record when I asked him to team with me in 1985 to start one of my companies, INJOY. In the beginning, we were long on potential and short on resources. Dick's hard work, planning, and insight turned a shoestring business operating out of his garage into an enterprise producing materials and influencing tens of thousands of leaders nationally and internationally every year. For fifteen years Dick served as the president of INJOY and helped get the company off the ground.

Management expert Robert Townsend notes, "Leaders come in all sizes, ages, shapes, and conditions. Some are poor administrators, some not overly bright. But there is one clue for spotting them. Since most people *per se* are mediocre, the true leader can be recognized because somehow or other, his people consistently turn in superior performances." Always check a candidate's past performance. A proven leader always has a proven track record.

7. CONFIDENCE

People will not follow a leader who does not have confidence in himself. In fact, people are naturally attracted to people who convey confidence. An excellent example can be seen in an incident in Russia during an attempted coup. Army tanks had surrounded the government building housing President Boris Yeltsin and his pro-democracy supporters. High-level military leaders had ordered the tank commander to open fire and kill Yeltsin. As the army rolled into position, Yeltsin strode from the building, climbed up on a tank, looked the commander in the eye, and thanked him for coming over to the side of democracy. Later the commander admitted that they had not intended to go over to his side. Yeltsin had appeared so confident and commanding that the soldiers talked after he left and decided to join him.

Confidence is characteristic of a positive attitude. The greatest achievers and leaders remain confident regardless of circumstances. Confidence is not simply for show. Confidence empowers. A *good* leader has the ability to instill within his people confidence in himself. A *great* leader has the ability to instill within his people confidence in themselves.

8. SELF-DISCIPLINE

Great leaders always have self-discipline—without exception. Unfortunately, our society seeks instant gratification rather than self-discipline. We want instant breakfast, fast food, movies on demand, and quick cash from ATMs. But success doesn't come instantly. Neither does the ability to lead. As General Dwight D. Eisenhower said, "There are no victories at bargain prices."

Because we live in a society of instant gratification, we cannot take for granted that the potential leaders we interview will have self-discipline—that they will be willing to pay the price of great leadership. When it comes to self-discipline, people choose one of two things: the pain of discipline that comes from sacrifice and growth, or the pain of regret that comes from the easy road and missed opportunities. Each person in life chooses. In *Adventures in Achievement*, E. James Rohn says that the pain of discipline weighs ounces. Regret weighs tons.

There are two areas of self-discipline we must look for in potential leaders we are considering equipping. The first is in the emotions. Effective leaders recognize that their emotional reactions are their own responsibility. A leader who decides not to allow other people's actions to dictate his reactions experiences an empowering freedom. As the Greek philosopher Epictetus said, "No person is free who is not master of himself."

The second area concerns time. Every person on the planet is given the same allotment of minutes in a day. But each person's level of self-discipline dictates how effectively those minutes are used. Disciplined people are always growing, always striving for improvement, and they maximize the use of their time. I have found three things that characterize disciplined leaders:

- They have identified specific long- and short-term goals for themselves.

- They have a plan for achieving those goals.

- They have a desire that motivates them to continue working to accomplish those goals.

Progress comes at a price. When you interview a potential leader, determine whether he or she is willing to pay the price. The author of the popular cartoon comic strip *Ziggy* recognized this when he drew the following scene:

As our friend Ziggy, in his little automobile, drove down a road, he saw two signs. The first stated in bold letters, THE ROAD TO SUCCESS. Farther down the road stood the second sign. It read, PREPARE TO STOP FOR TOLLS.

9. EFFECTIVE COMMUNICATION SKILLS

Never underestimate the importance of communication. It consumes enormous amounts of our time. One study, reported by D. K. Burlow in *The Process of Communication,* states that the average American spends 70 percent of his active hours each day communicating verbally. Without the ability to communicate, a leader cannot effectively cast his vision and call his people to act on that vision.

A leader's ability to convey confidence and his ability to communicate effectively are similar. Both require action on his part and a response from the follower. Communication is positive *interaction*. When communication is one-sided, it can be comical. You may have heard the story of the frustrated judge preparing to hear a divorce case:

"Why do you want a divorce?" the judge asked. "On what grounds?"

"All over. We have an acre and a half," responded the woman.

"No, no," said the judge. "Do you have a grudge?"

"Yes, sir. Fits two cars."

"I need a reason for the divorce," said the judge impatiently. "Does he beat you up?"

"Oh, no. I'm up at six every day to do my exercises. He gets up later."

"Please," said the exasperated judge. "What is the reason you want a divorce?"

"Oh," she replied. "We can't seem to communicate with each other."

When I look at a potential leader's communication skills, I look for the following:

A genuine concern for the person he's talking to. When people sense that you have a concern for them, they are willing to listen to what you have to say. Liking people is the beginning of the ability to communicate.

The ability to focus on the responder. Poor communicators are focused on themselves and their own opinions. Good communicators focus on the response of the person they're talking to. Good communicators also read body language.

The ability to communicate with all kinds of people. A good communicator has the ability to set a person at ease. She can find a way to relate to nearly anyone of any background.

Eye contact with the person he's speaking to. Most people who are being straight with you are willing to look you in the eye.

A warm smile. The fastest way to open the lines of communication is to smile. A smile overcomes innumerable communication barriers, crossing the boundaries of culture, race, age, class, gender, education, and economic status.

If I expect a person to lead, I must also expect him to be able to communicate.

10. Discontent with the Status Quo

I've told my staff before that *status quo* is Latin for "the mess we're in." Leaders see what is, but more important, they have vision for what could be. They are never content with things as they are. To be leading, by definition, is to be in front, breaking new ground, conquering new worlds, moving away from the status quo. Donna Harrison states, "Great leaders are never satisfied with current levels of performance. They constantly strive for higher and higher levels of achievement." They move beyond the status quo themselves, and they ask the same of those around them.

Dissatisfaction with the status quo does not mean a negative attitude or grumbling. It has to do with willingness to be different and take risks. A person who refuses to risk change fails to grow. A leader who loves the status quo soon becomes a follower. Raymond Smith, former CEO and Chairman of the Bell Atlantic Corporation, once remarked, "Taking the safe road, doing your job, and not making any waves may not get you fired (right away, at least), but it sure won't do much for your career or your company over the long haul. We're not dumb. We know that administrators are easy to find and cheap to keep. Leaders—risk takers—are in very short supply. And ones with vision are pure gold."

Risk seems dangerous to people more comfortable with old problems than new solutions. The difference between the energy and time that it takes to put up with the old problems and the energy and time it takes to come up with new solutions is surprisingly small. The difference is attitude. When seeking potential leaders, seek people who seek solutions.

Good leaders deliberately seek out and find potential leaders. Great leaders not only find them, but transform them into other great leaders. They have an ability to recognize ability and a strategy for finding leaders who make it happen. That's what takes their organizations to the next level.

5

What Does It Take to Equip a Leader?

Equipping, like nurturing, is an ongoing process.

Equipping is similar to training. But I prefer the term "equipping" because it more accurately describes the process potential leaders must go through. Training is generally focused on specific job tasks; for instance, you train a person to use a copy machine or to answer a phone in a particular way. Training is only a part of the equipping process that prepares a person for leadership.

When I think of equipping a potential leader, I think of preparing an unskilled person to scale a tall mountain peak. His preparation is a process. Certainly he needs to be outfitted with equipment, such as cold-weather clothing, ropes, picks, and spikes. He also needs to be trained how to use that equipment.

A mountain climber's preparation, though, involves much more than simply having the correct equipment and knowing how to use it. The person must be conditioned physically to prepare him for the difficult climb. He must be trained to be a part of a team. Most important, he must be taught to *think* like a mountain climber. He needs to be able to look at a peak and *see* how it is to be conquered. Without going through the complete equipping process, he not only won't make it to the top of the mountain, but he also might find himself stranded on the side of the mountain, freezing to death.

Equipping, like nurturing, is an ongoing process. You don't equip a person in a few hours or a day. And it can't be done using a formula or a videotape. Equipping must be tailored to each potential leader.

EQUIPPING IS AN ONGOING PROCESS.

YOUR ROLE AS EQUIPPER

The ideal equipper is a person who can impart the vision of the work, evaluate the potential leader, give him the tools he needs, and then help him along the way at the beginning of his journey.

The equipper is a *model*—a leader who does the job, does it well, does it right, and does it with consistency.

The equipper is a *mentor*—an advisor who has the vision of the organization and can communicate it to others. He or she has experience to draw upon.

The equipper is an *empowerer*—one who can instill in the potential leader the desire and ability to do the work. He or she is able to lead, teach, and assess the progress of the person being equipped.

The steps that follow will take you through the whole process. They begin with building a relationship with your potential leaders. From that foundation, you can build a program for their development, supervise their progress, empower them to do the job, and finally get them to pass on the legacy.

DEVELOP A PERSONAL RELATIONSHIP WITH THE PEOPLE YOU EQUIP

All good mentoring relationships begin with personal relationships. As your people get to know and like you, their desire to follow your direction and learn from you will increase. If they don't like you, they will not want to learn from you, and the equipping process slows down or even stops.

To build relationships, begin by listening to people's life stories, their journeys so far. Your genuine interest in them will mean a lot to them. It will also help you to know their personal strengths and weaknesses. Ask them about their goals and what motivates them. Find out what kind of temperament they have. If you first find their hearts, they'll be glad to give you their hands.

ALL GOOD MENTORING RELATIONSHIPS BEGIN
WITH PERSONAL RELATIONSHIPS.

SHARE YOUR DREAM

While getting to know your people, share your dream. It helps them to know you and where you're going. There's no act that will better show them your heart and your motivation.

Woodrow Wilson once said, "We grow by dreams. All big individuals are dreamers. They see things in the soft haze of a spring day, or in the red fire on a long winter's evening. Some of us let those great dreams die, but others nourish and protect them; nourish them through bad days until they bring them to the sunshine and light which comes always to those who sincerely hope that their dreams will come true." I have often wondered, "Does the person make the dream or does the dream make the person?" My conclusion is both are equally true.

All good leaders have a dream. All great leaders share their dream with others who can help them make it a reality. As Florence Littauer suggests, we must

Dare to dream: Have the desire to do something
                     bigger than yourself.

Prepare the dream: Do your homework; be ready when the opportunity comes.

Wear the dream: Do it.

Share the dream: Make others a part of the dream, and it will become even greater than you had hoped.

ASK FOR COMMITMENT

In his book *The One Minute Manager*, Ken Blanchard says, "There's a difference between interest and commitment. When you are interested in doing something, you do it only when it is convenient. When you are committed to something, you accept no excuses." Don't equip people who are merely interested. Equip the ones who are committed.

To determine whether your people are committed, first you must make sure they know what it will cost them to become leaders. That means that you must be sure not to undersell the job—let them know what it's going to take. If they won't commit, don't go any further in the equipping process. Don't waste your time.

SET GOALS FOR GROWTH

People need clear objectives set before them if they are to achieve anything of value. Success never comes instantaneously. It comes from taking many small steps. A set of goals becomes a map a potential leader can follow in order to grow. As Shad Helmsetter states in *You Can Excel in Time of Change*, "It is the goal that shapes the plan; it is the plan that sets the action; it is the action that achieves the result; and it is the result that brings the success. And it all begins with the simple word *goal.*" We, as equipping leaders, must introduce our people to the practice of setting and achieving goals.

When you help your people set goals, use the following guidelines:

Make the goals appropriate. Always keep in mind the job you want the people to do and the desired result: the development of your people into effective leaders. Identify goals that will contribute to that larger goal.

Make the goals attainable. Nothing will make people want to quit faster than facing unachievable goals. I like the comment made by Ian MacGregor, former AMAX Corporation chairman of the board: "I work on the same principle as people who train horses. You start with low fences, easily achieved goals, and work up. It's important in management never to ask people to try to accomplish goals they can't accept."

Make the goals measurable. Your potential leaders will never know when they have achieved their goals if they aren't measurable. When they are measurable, the knowledge that they have been attained will give them a sense of accomplishment. It will also free them to set new goals in place of the old ones.

Clearly state the goal. When goals have no clear focus, neither will the actions of the people trying to achieve them.

Make the goals require a "stretch." As I mentioned before, goals have to be achievable. On the other hand, when goals don't require a stretch, the people achieving them won't grow. The leader must know his people well enough to identify attainable goals that require a stretch.

Put the goals in writing. When people write down their goals, it makes them more accountable for those goals. A study of a Yale University graduating class showed that the small percentage of graduates who had written down their goals accomplished more than all of the other graduates combined. Putting goals in writing works.

COMMUNICATE THE FUNDAMENTALS

For people to be productive and satisfied professionally, they have to know what their fundamental responsibilities are. It sounds so simple, but Peter Drucker says one of the critical problems in the workplace today is that there is a lack of understanding between the employer and employee as to what the employee is to do. Often employees are made to feel they are vaguely responsible for everything. It paralyzes them. Instead, we need to make clear to them what they *are* and *are not* responsible for. Then they will be able to focus their efforts on what we want, and they will succeed.

Look again at how a basketball team works. Each of the five players has a particular job. There is a shooting guard whose job is to score points. The other guard is a point guard. His job is to pass the ball to people who can score. Another player is a power forward who is expected to get rebounds. The small forward's job is to score. The center is supposed to rebound, block shots, and score. Each person on the team knows what his job is, what his unique contribution to the team must be. When each concentrates on his particular responsibilities, the team can win.

Finally, a leader must communicate to his or her people that their work has value to the organization and to the individual leader. To the employee, this often is the most important fundamental of all.

PERFORM THE FIVE-STEP PROCESS OF TRAINING PEOPLE

Part of the equipping process includes training people to perform the specific tasks of the jobs they are to do. The approach the leader takes to training will largely determine his people's success or failure. If he takes a dry, academic approach, the potential leaders will remember little of what's taught.

The best type of training takes advantage of the way

people learn. Researchers tell us that we remember 10 percent of what we hear, 50 percent of what we see, 70 percent of what we say, and 90 percent of what we hear, see, say, and do. Knowing that, we have to develop an approach to how we will train. I have found the best training method to be a five-step process:

Step 1: I model. The process begins with my doing the tasks while the people being trained watch. When I do this, I try to give them an opportunity to see me go through the whole process.

Step 2: I mentor. During this next step, I continue to perform the task, but this time the person I'm training comes alongside me and assists in the process. I also take time to explain not only the *how* but also the *why* of each step.

Step 3: I monitor. We exchange places this time. The trainee performs the task and I assist and correct. It's especially important during this phase to be positive and encouraging to the trainee. It keeps him trying and it makes him want to improve rather than give up. Work with him until he develops consistency. Once he's gotten down the process, ask him to explain it to you. It will help him to understand and remember.

Step 4: I motivate. I take myself out of the task at this point and let the trainee go. My task is to make sure he knows how to do it without help and to keep encouraging him so he will continue to improve. It is important for me to stay with him until he senses success. It's a great motivator. At this time the trainee may want to make improvements to the process. Encourage him to do it, and at the same time learn from him.

Step 5: I multiply. This is my favorite part of the whole process. Once the new leaders do the job well, it becomes their turn to teach others how to do it. As teachers know, the best way to learn something is to teach it. And the beauty of this is it frees me to do other important developmental tasks while others carry on the training.

GIVE THE "BIG THREE"

All the training in the world will provide limited success if you don't turn your people loose to do the job. I believe that if I get the best people, give them my vision, train them in the basics, and then let go, I will get a high return from them. As General George S. Patton once remarked, "Never tell people how to do things. Tell them what to do and they will surprise you with their ingenuity."

You can't turn people loose without structure, but you also want to give them enough freedom to be creative. The way to do that is to give them the big three: *responsibility, authority,* and *accountability.*

What is difficult for some leaders is allowing their people to keep the responsibility after it's been given. Poor managers want to control every detail of their people's work. When that happens, the potential leaders who work for them become frustrated and don't develop. Rather than desiring more responsibility, they become indifferent or avoid responsibility altogether. If you want your people to take responsibility, truly give it to them.

With responsibility must go authority. Progress does not come unless they are given together. Winston Churchill, while addressing the House of Commons during the Second World War, said, "I am your servant. You have the right to dismiss me when you please. What you have no right to do is ask me to bear responsibility without the power of action." When responsibility and authority come together, people become genuinely empowered.

There's an important aspect of authority that needs to be noted. When we first give authority to new leaders, we are actually *giving them permission* to have authority rather than *giving them authority* itself. True authority has to be earned.

We must give our people permission to develop authority. That is our responsibility. They, in turn, must take responsibility for earning it.

I have found there are different levels of authority:

Position. The most basic kind of authority comes from a person's position on the organizational chart. This type of authority does not extend beyond the parameters of the job description. This is where all new leaders start. From here they may either earn greater authority, or they can minimize what little authority they have been given. It's up to them.

Competence. This type of authority is based on a person's professional capabilities, the ability to do a job. Followers give competent leaders authority within their area of expertise.

Personality. Followers will also give authority to people based on their personal characteristics, such as personality, appearance, and charisma. Authority based on personality is a little broader than competence-based authority, but it is not really more advanced because it tends to be superficial.

Integrity. Authority based on integrity comes from a person's core. It is based on character. When new leaders gain authority based on their integrity, they have crossed into a new stage of their development.

Spirituality. In secular circles, people rarely consider the power of spiritual-based authority. It comes from people's individual experiences with God and from His power working through them. It is the highest form of authority.

Leaders must earn authority with each new group of people. However, I have found that once leaders have gained authority on a particular level, it takes very little time for them to establish that level of authority with another group of people. The higher the level of authority, the more quickly it happens.

Once responsibility and authority have been given to people, they are empowered to make things happen. But we also have to be sure they are making the right things happen. That's where accountability comes into the picture. If we are providing them the right climate, our people will not fear accountability. They will admit mistakes and see them as a part of the learning process.

The leader's part of accountability involves taking the time to review the new leader's work and give honest, constructive criticism. It is crucial that the leader be supportive but honest. It's been said that when Harry Truman was thrust into the presidency upon the death of President Franklin D. Roosevelt, Speaker of the House Sam Rayburn gave him some fatherly advice: "From here on out you're going to have lots of people around you. They'll try to put a wall around you and cut you off from any ideas but theirs. They'll tell you what a great man you are, Harry. But you and I both know you ain't." Rayburn was holding President Truman accountable.

GIVE THEM THE TOOLS THEY NEED

Giving responsibility without resources is ridiculous; it is incredibly limiting. Abraham Maslow said, "If the only tool you have is a hammer, you tend to see every problem as a nail." If we want our people to be creative and resourceful, we need to provide resources.

Obviously, the most basic tools are pieces of equipment, such as copying machines, computers, and whatever else simplifies someone's work. We must be sure not only to provide everything necessary for a job to be done, but also equipment that will allow jobs, especially "B" priorities, to be done more quickly and efficiently. Always work toward freeing people's time for important things.

Tools, however, include much more than equipment. It is important to provide developmental tools. Spend time mentoring people in specific areas of need. Be willing to spend money on things like books, tapes, seminars, and professional conferences. There is a wealth of good information out there, and fresh ideas from outside an organization can stimulate growth. Be creative in providing tools. It will keep your people growing and equip them to do the job well.

CHECK ON THEM SYSTEMATICALLY

I believe in touching base with people frequently. I like to give mini-evaluations all the time. Leaders who wait to give feedback only during annual formal evaluations are asking for trouble. People need the encouragement of being told they're doing well on a regular basis. They also need to hear as soon as possible when they are not doing well. It prevents a lot of problems with the organization, and it improves the leader.

How often I check on people is determined by a number of factors:

The importance of the task. When something is critical to the success of the organization, I touch base often.

The demands of the work. I find that if the work is very demanding, the person performing it needs encouragement more often.

The newness of the work. Some leaders have no problem tackling a new task, no matter how different it is from previous work. Others have great difficulty adapting. I check often on the people who are less flexible or creative.

The newness of the worker. I want to give new leaders every possible chance to succeed. So I check on newer people more often. That way I can help them anticipate problems and make sure that they have a series of successes. By that they gain confidence.

The responsibility of the worker. When I know I can give a person a task and it will always get done, I may not check on that person until the task is complete. With less responsible people, I can't afford to do that.

My approach to checking on people also varies from person to person. For instance, rookies and veterans should be treated differently. But no matter how long people have been with me, there are some things I always do: Discuss feelings; measure progress; give feedback; and give encouragement.

Though it doesn't happen very often, I occasionally have a person whose progress is repeatedly poor. When that happens, I try to determine what's gone wrong. Usually poor performance is a result of one of three things: (1) a mismatch between the job and the person; (2) inadequate training or leadership; or (3) deficiencies in the person performing the work. Before I take any action, I always try to determine what the issues are. I line up my facts to be sure there really is a deficiency in performance and not just a problem with my perception. Next I define as precisely as possible what the deficiency is. Finally, I check with the person who is not performing to get the other side of the story.

Once I've done my homework, I try to determine where the deficiency is. If it's a mismatch, I explain the problem to the person, move him to a place that fits, and reassure him of my confidence in him.

If the problem involves training or leadership issues, I back up and redo whatever step hasn't been performed properly. Once again, I let the person know what the problem was and give him plenty of encouragement.

If the problem is with the person, I sit down with him and let him know about it. I make it clear where his failures are and what he must do to overcome them. Then I give him another chance. But I also begin the documentation process in case I have to fire him. I want him to succeed, but I will waste no time letting him go if he doesn't do what it takes to improve.

CONDUCT PERIODIC EQUIPPING MEETINGS

Even after you've completed most of your people's training and are preparing to take them into their next growth phase—development—continue to conduct periodic equipping meetings. It helps your people stay on track, helps them keep growing, and encourages them to begin taking responsibility for equipping themselves.

When I prepare an equipping meeting, I include the following:

Good news. I always start on a positive note. I review the good things that are happening in the organization and pay particular attention to their areas of interest and responsibility.

Vision. People can get so caught up in their day-to-day responsibilities that they lose sight of the vision that drives the organization. Use the opportunity of an equipping meeting to recast that vision.

Content. Content will depend on their needs. Try to focus training on areas that will help them in the priority areas, and orient the training on the people, not the lesson.

Administration. Cover any organizational items that give the people a sense of security and encourage their leadership.

Empowerment. Take time to connect with the people you

equip. Encourage them personally. And show them how the equipping session empowers them to perform their jobs better. They will leave the meeting feeling positive and ready to work.

The entire equipping process takes a lot of time and attention. It requires more time and dedication from the equipping leader than mere training. But its focus is long term, not short term. Rather than creating followers or even adding new leaders, it *multiplies* leaders. As I explained earlier, it is not complete until the equipper and the new leader select someone for the new leader to train. It is only then that the equipping process has come full circle. Without a successor, there can be no success.

PART III

EQUIPPING FOR THE NEXT LEVEL

HOW CAN A LEADER INSPIRE OTHERS TO EXCEL?

Adding value is really the essence of equipping others.

In 1296, King Edward I of England assembled a large army and crossed the border of his own nation into Scotland. Edward was a skilled leader and fierce warrior. A tall, strong man, he had gained his first real combat experience beginning at age twenty-five. In the following years, he became a seasoned veteran while fighting in the Crusades in the Holy Lands.

At age fifty-seven, he was fresh from victories in Wales, whose people he'd crushed and whose land he'd annexed. In that conflict, his purpose had been clear: He said it was "to check the impetuous rashness of the Welsh, to punish their presumption and to wage war against them to their extermination."[1]

Edward's invasion of Scotland was intended to break the will of the Scottish people once and for all. Previously, he had managed to make himself overlord of the territory and then placed a weak king over it, a man the people of Scotland called Toom Tabard, meaning "empty coat." Then Edward bullied the straw king until he rebelled, thus giving the English monarch a reason to invade the country. The Scottish people crumpled.

A BOLD LEADER EMERGED

Edward sacked the castle of Berwick and massacred its inhabitants. Other castles surrendered in quick succession. The Scottish king was stripped of power, and many believed that the fate of the Scots would be the same as that of the Welsh. But they didn't take into account the efforts of one man: Sir William Wallace, who is still revered as a national hero in Scotland even though he has been dead for nearly seven hundred years.

If you saw the movie *Braveheart,* then you have an image of William Wallace as a fierce and determined fighter who valued freedom above all else. His older brother, Malcolm, as the firstborn son, was expected to follow in the footsteps of their father as a warrior. William, as many second sons of the day, was instead groomed for the clergy. He was taught to value ideas, including freedom. But Wallace grew to resent the oppressive English rulers after his father was killed in an ambush and his mother was forced to live in exile. At age nineteen, he became a fighter when a group of Englishmen tried to bully him. By his early twenties, William Wallace was a highly skilled warrior.

The People Went to a Higher Level

During the time of William Wallace and Edward I, warfare was usually conducted by trained knights, professional soldiers, and sometimes hired mercenaries. The larger and more seasoned the army, the greater their power. When Edward faced the smaller Welsh army, they didn't stand a chance. And the same was expected of the Scots. But Wallace had an unusual ability. He drew the common people of Scotland to him, he made them believe in the cause of freedom, and he inspired and equipped them to fight against the professional war machine of England. He enlarged their vision and their abilities.

William Wallace was ultimately unable to defeat the English and gain Scotland's independence. At age thirty-three, he was brutally executed. (His treatment was actually worse than that portrayed in the movie *Braveheart*.) But his legacy of enlargement carried on. The next year, inspired by Wallace's example, nobleman Robert Bruce claimed the throne of Scotland and rallied not only the peasants but also the nobility. And in 1314, Scotland finally gained its hard-fought independence.

CHARACTERISTICS OF ENLARGING LEADERS

Team members always love and admire a player who is able to help them go to another level, someone who enlarges them and empowers them to be successful. Those kinds of people are like the Boston Celtics Hall of Fame center Bill Russell, who said, "The most important measure of how good a game I played was how much better I'd made my teammates play."

Leaders who enlarge their teammates have several things in common:

THEY VALUE THEIR TEAM MEMBERS

Industrialist Charles Schwab observed, "I have yet to find the man, however exalted his station, who did not do better work and put forth greater effort under a spirit of approval than under a spirit of criticism." Your team members can tell whether you believe in them. People's performances usually reflect the expectations of those they respect.

"THE MOST IMPORTANT MEASURE OF HOW GOOD A GAME
I PLAYED WAS HOW MUCH BETTER I'D MADE
MY TEAMMATES PLAY."—BILL RUSSELL

They Value What Their Team Members Value

Players who enlarge others do more than value their fellow team members; they understand what their team members value. They listen to discover what they talk about and watch to see what they spend their money on. That kind of knowledge, along with a desire to relate to their fellow players, creates a strong connection between them. And it makes possible an enlarger's next characteristic.

They Add Value to Their Team Members

Adding value is really the essence of enlarging others. It's finding ways to help others improve their abilities and attitudes. A leader who equips and enlarges others looks for the gifts, talents, and uniqueness in other people, and then helps them to increase those abilities for their benefit and for that of the entire team. An enlarging leader is able to take others to a whole new level.

They Make Themselves More Valuable

Enlargers work to make themselves better, not only because it benefits them personally, but also because it helps them to help others. You cannot give what you do not have. If you want to increase the ability of your team members, make yourself better.

HOW TO BECOME AN ENLARGER

If you want to be an enlarging team leader, then do the following:

1. BELIEVE IN OTHERS BEFORE THEY BELIEVE IN YOU

If you want to help people become better, you need to become an initiator. You can't hold back. Ask yourself, What is special, unique, and wonderful about that team member? Then share your observations with the person and with others. If you believe in others and give them a positive reputation to uphold, you can help them to become better than they think they are.

2. SERVE OTHERS BEFORE THEY SERVE YOU

One of the most beneficial services you can perform is helping other human beings to reach their potential. In your family, serve your spouse. In business, help your colleagues to shine. And whenever possible, give credit to others for the team's success.

3. ADD VALUE TO OTHERS BEFORE THEY ADD VALUE TO YOU

A basic truth of life is that people will always move toward anyone who increases them and away from others who devalue them. You can enlarge others by pointing out their strengths and helping them to focus on improvement.

For as long as he could remember, a boy named Chris Greicius dreamed of someday becoming a police officer. But there was a major obstacle standing in his way. He had leukemia, and he was not expected to make it to adulthood. When he was seven years old, Chris's battle with the disease took a turn for the worse, and that's when a family friend, who was a U.S. customs officer, arranged for Chris to come as close as he could to living his dream. He made a call to Officer Ron Cox in Phoenix and arranged for Chris to spend the day with officers from the Arizona Department of Public Safety.

A BASIC TRUTH OF LIFE IS THAT PEOPLE WILL ALWAYS
MOVE TOWARD ANYONE WHO INCREASES THEM
AND AWAY FROM OTHERS WHO DEVALUE THEM.

When the day arrived, Chris was welcomed by three squad cars and a police motorcycle ridden by Frank Shankwitz. Then he was treated to a ride in a police helicopter. They finished the day by swearing Chris in as the first—and only—honorary state trooper. The next day, Cox enlisted the assistance of the company that manufactured the uniforms for the Arizona Highway Patrol, and within twenty-four hours, their people presented Chris with an official patrolman's uniform. He was ecstatic.

Two days later, Chris died in the hospital, his uniform close at hand. Officer Shankwitz was saddened by his little friend's death, but he was grateful that he had experienced the opportunity to help Chris. And he also realized that there were many children in circumstances similar to Chris's. That prompted Shankwitz to cofound the Make-A-Wish Foundation. In twenty years since then, he and his organization have enlarged the experiences of more than eighty thousand children.

There is nothing as valuable—or rewarding—as adding value to the lives of others. When you help others to go to another level, you go to another level yourself.

HOW CAN I HELP OTHERS FULFILL THEIR POTENTIAL?

*Having the right people
in the right places is essential to
individual and team success.*

I f you succeed in developing people in your organization and equipping them to lead, you will be successful. If you enlarge them and motivate them to achieve, they will be grateful to you as their leader. And to be honest, you will have done more than many other leaders do. However, you can take yet another step that will help someone you equip to fulfill their potential. You can help them to find their niche in life. Good things happen when a player takes the place where he or she adds the most value. Great things happen when all the players on the team take the roles that maximize their strengths—their talent, skill, and experience. It takes every individual—and the whole team—to a whole new level.

WHEN PEOPLE ARE IN THE WRONG PLACE

Just about everyone has experienced being on some kind of team where people had to take on roles that didn't suit them: an accountant forced to work with people all day, a basketball forward forced to play center, a guitarist filling in on keyboard, a teacher stuck doing paperwork, a spouse who hates the kitchen taking on the role of cook.

What happens to a team when one or more of its members constantly play "out of position"? First, morale erodes because the team isn't playing up to its capability. Then people become resentful. The people working in an area of weakness resent that their best is untapped. And other people on the team who know that they could better fill a mismatched position on the team resent that their skills are being overlooked. Before long, people become unwilling to work as a team. Then everyone's confidence begins to erode. And the situation just keeps getting worse. The team stops progressing, and the competition takes advantage of the team's obvious weaknesses. As a result, the team never realizes its potential. When people aren't where they do things well, things don't turn out well—for the individual or for the team.

Having the right people in the right places is essential to individual and team success. Take a look at how a team's dynamic changes according to the placement of people:

The Wrong Person in the Wrong Place = Regression

The Wrong Person in the Right Place = Frustration

The Right Person in the Wrong Place = Confusion

The Right Person in the Right Place = Progression

The Right People in the Right Places = Multiplication

It doesn't matter what kind of team you're dealing with: the principles are the same. David Ogilvy was right when he said, "A well-run restaurant is like a winning baseball team. It makes the most of every crew member's talent and takes advantage of every split-second opportunity to speed up service."

A few years ago I was asked to write a chapter for a book called *Destiny and Deliverance,* which was tied to the Dreamworks movie *The Prince of Egypt.* It was a wonderful experience, which I greatly enjoyed. During the writing process, I was invited to go to California and view parts of the movie while it was still in production. That made me want to do something I had never done before: attend a movie premiere in Hollywood.

My publisher managed to get me a pair of tickets for the premiere, and when the time arrived, my wife, Margaret, and I went out for the event. It was a blast. It was a high-energy event filled with movie stars and moviemakers. Margaret and I enjoyed the movie—and the whole experience—immensely.

Now, anybody who's gone to a movie, show, or sporting event with me knows my pattern. As soon as I am pretty certain about the outcome of a ball game, I hit the exit to beat the crowds. When the Broadway audience is giving the ovation, I'm gone. And the second the credits begin to roll in a movie, I'm out of my seat. As *The Prince of Egypt* came to a close, I started to get ready to get up, but not a person in the theater moved. And then something really surprising happened. As the credits rolled, people began to applaud the lesser known individuals whose names appeared on the screen: the costume designer, the gaffer, the key grip, the assistant director. It was a moment I'll never forget—and a great reminder that all players have a place where they add the most value. That not only helps people to reach their potential, but it builds the team. When each person does the job that's best for him or her, everybody wins.

TO PUT PEOPLE IN THEIR PLACE

NFL champion coach Vince Lombardi observed, "The achievements of an organization are the results of the combined effort of each individual." That is true, but creating a winning team doesn't come just from having the right individuals. Even if you have a great group of talented individuals, if each person is not doing what adds the most value to the team, you won't achieve your potential as a team. That's the art of leading a team. You've got to put people in their place—and I mean that in the most positive way!

To take people to the next level by putting them in the places that utilize their talents and maximize the team's potential, you need three things. You must . . .

1. Know the Team

You cannot build a winning team or organization if you don't know its vision, purpose, culture, or history. If you don't know where the team is trying to go—and why it's trying to get there—you cannot bring the team to the height of its potential. You've got to start where the team actually is; only then can you take it somewhere.

2. Know the Situation

Even though the vision or purpose of an organization may be fairly constant, its situation changes constantly. Good team builders know where the team is and what the situation requires. For example, when a team is young and just getting started, the greatest priority is often to just get good people.

But as a team matures and the level of talent increases, then fine-tuning becomes more important. It's at that time that a leader must spend more time matching the person to the position.

3. KNOW THE PLAYER

It sounds obvious, but you must know the person you are trying to position in the right niche. I mention it because leaders tend to want to make everyone else conform to their image, to approach their work using the same skills and problem-solving methods. But team building is not working on an assembly line.

Mother Teresa, who worked with people her whole life, observed, "I can do what you can't do, and you can do what I can't do; together we can do great things." As you work to build a team, look at each person's experience, skills, temperament, attitude, passion, people skills, discipline, emotional strength, and potential. Only then will you be ready to help a team member to find his or her proper place.

"I CAN DO WHAT YOU CAN'T DO, AND YOU CAN DO WHAT
I CAN'T DO; TOGETHER WE CAN DO GREAT THINGS."
—MOTHER TERESA

Start by Finding the Right Place for You

Right now you may not be in a position to place others on your team. In fact, you may be thinking to yourself, *How do I find my own niche?* If that's the case, then follow these guidelines:

- BE SECURE: My friend Wayne Schmidt says, "No amount of personal competency compensates for personal insecurity." If you allow your insecurities to get the better of you, you'll be inflexible and reluctant to change. And you cannot grow with change.

- GET TO KNOW YOURSELF: You won't be able to find your niche if you don't know your strengths and weaknesses. Spend time reflecting and exploring your gifts. Ask others to give you feedback. Do what it takes to remove personal blind spots.

- TRUST YOUR LEADER: A good leader will help you to start moving in the right direction. If you don't trust your leader, look to another mentor for help. Or get on another team.

- SEE THE BIG PICTURE: Your place on the team only makes sense in the context of the big picture. If your only motivation for finding your niche is personal gain, your poor motives may prevent you from discovering what you desire.

• RELY ON YOUR EXPERIENCE: When it comes down to it, the only way to know that you've discovered your niche is to try what seems right and learn from your failures and successes. When you discover what you were made for, your heart sings. It says, *There's no place like this place anywhere near this place, so this must be the place!*

A PLACE FOR EVERYONE, AND EVERYONE IN HIS PLACE

One organization that strives to match its people to the right place is the U.S. military. That is particularly true now that it employs an all-volunteer force. If each of the various functions in a military command don't work at top efficiency (and interact well with all the other parts), then terrible breakdowns occur.

WHEN YOU DISCOVER YOUR PLACE YOU WILL SAY, "THERE'S NO PLACE LIKE THIS PLACE ANYWHERE NEAR THIS PLACE, SO THIS MUST BE THE PLACE!"

Nobody is more keenly aware of that than a combat pilot. Take for example Charlie Plumb who retired as a captain of the U.S. Navy. A graduate of Annapolis, he served in Vietnam in the mid-sixties, flying seventy-five missions from the aircraft carrier USS *Kitty Hawk*.

An aircraft carrier is a place where you can readily observe how all the pieces of the military "puzzle" come together to support each other. A carrier is often described as being like a floating city. It contains a crew of 5,500 people, a population greater than that of some of the towns in which its crew members grew up. It must be self-sustaining, and each of its seventeen departments must function as a team accomplishing its mission. And those teams must work together as a team.

Every pilot is acutely aware of the team effort required to put a jet in the air. It takes hundreds of people utilizing dozens of technical specialties to launch, monitor, support, land, and maintain an aircraft. Even more people are involved if that plane is armed for combat. Charlie Plumb was undoubtedly aware that many people worked tirelessly to keep him flying. But despite the efforts of the best-trained air support group in the world, Plumb found himself in a North Vietnamese prison as a POW after his F-4 Phantom jet was shot down on May 19, 1967, during his seventy-fifth mission.

Plumb was held prisoner for nearly six grueling years, part of the time in the infamous Hanoi Hilton. During those years he and his fellow prisoners were humiliated, starved, tortured, and forced to live in squalid conditions. Yet he didn't let the experience break him. He now says, "Our unity through our faith in God and in our love for Country were the great strength which kept us going through some very difficult times."

TURNING POINT

Plumb was released from his imprisonment on February 18, 1973, and continued his career in the navy. But an incident years after his return to the United States marked his life as surely as his imprisonment. One day he and his wife, Cathy, were eating in a restaurant when a man came to the table and said, "You're Plumb. You flew jet fighters in Vietnam."

"That's right," answered Plumb, "I did."

"It was fighter squadron 114 on the *Kitty Hawk*. You were shot down. You were parachuted into enemy hands," the man continued. "You spent six years as a prisoner of war."

The former pilot was taken aback. He looked at the man, trying to identify him, but couldn't. "How in the world did you know that?" Plumb finally asked.

"I packed your parachute."

Plumb was staggered. All he could do was struggle to his feet and shake the man's hand. "I must tell you," Plumb finally said, "I've said a lot of prayers of thanks for your nimble fingers, but I didn't realize I'd have the opportunity of saying thanks in person."[1]

What if the navy had put the wrong person in the position of parachute rigger, the anonymous and the rarely thanked job that man performed during the Vietnam War? Charlie Plumb wouldn't have known about it until it was too late. And we wouldn't even know where the breakdown had occurred, because Plumb wouldn't have lived to tell the tale.

Today, Charlie Plumb is a motivational speaker to Fortune 500 companies, government agencies, and other organizations. He often tells the story of the man who packed his parachute, and he uses it to deliver a message on teamwork. He says, "In a world where downsizing forces us to do more with less, we must empower the team. 'Packing others' parachutes' can mean the difference in survival. Yours and your team's!"[2]

If you desire to pack the parachutes of your people, after you equip them, find the niche where they will flourish. That is the best way to empower them. They will grow to their potential, and your team will go to a whole new level.

NOTES

Chapter 2
1. Don Banks, "Teacher First, Seldom Second, Wootten Has Built Monument to Excellence at Maryland's DeMatha High," *St. Petersburg Times*, 3 April 1987, www.dematha.org.
2. John Feinstein, "A Down-to-Earth Coach Brings DeMatha to New Heights," *Washington Post*, 27 February 1984, www.dematha.org.
3. Morgan Wootten and Bill Gilbert, *From Orphans to Champions: The Story of DeMatha's Morgan Wootten* (New York: Atheneum, 1979), 24–25.
4. William Plummer, "Wootten's Way," *People*, 20 November 2000, 166.
5. Wootten and Gilbert, *From Orphans to Champions*, 12–13.

Chapter 4
1. John C. Maxwell, *The Winning Attitude: Your Key to Personal Success* (Nashville, Tennessee: Thomas Nelson, 1993).

Chapter 6
1. "Edwardian Conquest," 14 June 2001,
   www.britannia.com/wales.

Chapter 7
1. "Packing Parachutes," audiotape excerpt,
   <www.charlieplumb.com>.
2. "Charlie Plumb's Speech Content,"
   <www.charlieplumb.com>.

ATTITUDE

101

WHAT EVERY LEADER NEEDS TO KNOW

JOHN C. MAXWELL

NELSON BUSINESS
A Division of Thomas Nelson Publishers
Since 1798

www.thomasnelson.com

Published in Nashville, Tennessee, by Thomas Nelson, Inc.

Unless otherwise noted, Scripture quotations are from
THE NEW KING JAMES VERSION
of the Bible. Copyright © 1979, 1980, 1982,
Thomas Nelson, Inc., Publishers.

Scripture quotations noted NIV are from the HOLY BIBLE: NEW
INTERNATIONAL VERSION®. Copyright © 1973, 1978, 1984 by
International Bible Society. Used by permission of Zondervan
Publishing House. All rights reserved.

Portions of this book were previously published in *The Winning
Attitude, Failing Forward, Your Roadmap for Success, The 17 Indisputable
Laws of Teamwork,* and *The 21 Irrefutable Laws of Leadership.*

Library of Congress Cataloging-in-Publication Data

Maxwell, John C., 1947–
Attitude 101 / John C. Maxwell.
p. cm.
ISBN 0-7852-6350-0 (hardcover)
1. Success—Psychological aspects. 2. Attitude (Psychology). I. Title.
BF637.S8 M3415 2002
153.8'5—dc21
2002011491

Contents

Publisher's Preface

Who cares about a person's attitude? As long as someone can do the job, you shouldn't worry too much about it, right? If John Maxwell believed that, you wouldn't have *Attitude 101* in your hands right now.

As America's leadership expert, Dr. Maxwell has devoted his life to helping people become more successful. His books and seminars teach that anyone can be a REAL success if they master skills in four areas: Relationships, Equipping, Attitude, and Leadership. This book is designed to give you the essentials of attitude—in a quick, easy-to-read format.

People's lives are so hectic. Their time is valuable, and yet, they are also on information overload. More new information has been produced in the last thirty years than in the previous five thousand. A weekday edition of the *New York Times* contains more information than average people in seventeenth-century England were likely to come across in their lifetime. The amount of information available in the world has doubled in the last five years, and it will keep doubling.

So this book, a companion to *Leadership 101*, *Relationships 101* (available January 2004), and *Equipping 101* (available January 2004), is the short course on attitude. Dr. Maxwell recognizes that as an individual, your attitude has a profound impact on your life. As a leader, you cannot ignore the attitudes of the people you lead and expect to achieve success—whether you're leading a business, a family, a sports team, or a group of volunteers. A person's attitude impacts their relationships, colors their view of failure, and defines their approach to success. Attitude can make or break you.

We are delighted to publish *Attitude 101* because we realize that few things in life are a greater asset than an attitude of positive determination. *Attitude 101* is designed to empower you and your team to succeed by helping you become equipped with the right kind of attitude. Here's to your success—and to your reaching the next level!

PART I

THE IMPACT OF ATTITUDE

I

How Does Attitude Impact Leadership?

Attitude is always a "player" on your team.

Growing up, I loved basketball. It all started for me in the fourth grade when I saw a high school basketball game for the first time. I was captivated. After that, I could usually be found practicing my shooting and playing pickup games on my small court at home.

By the time I got to high school, I had become a pretty good player. I started on the junior varsity team as a freshman, and when I was a sophomore, our JV team had a 15-3 record, which was better than that of the varsity. We were proud of our performance—maybe a little too proud.

The next year, critics who followed high school basketball in Ohio thought our team had a chance to win the state championship in our division. I guess they looked at the players who would return as seniors from the previous year's varsity team, saw the talent that would be moving up from the JV, and figured we would be a powerhouse. And we did have a lot of talent. How many high school teams in the late 1960s could say that all but a couple of players on the team could dunk the ball? But the season turned out far different from everyone's expectations.

FROM BAD TO WORSE

From the beginning of the season, the team suffered problems. There were two of us juniors on the varsity who had the talent to start for the team: John Thomas, who was the team's best rebounder, and me, the best shooting guard. We thought playing time should be based strictly on ability, and we figured we deserved our place on the team. The seniors, who had taken a backseat to the previous year's seniors, thought we should be made to pay our dues and wait on the bench.

What began as a rivalry between the JV and varsity the year before turned into a war between the juniors and the seniors. When we scrimmaged at practice, it was the juniors against the seniors. In games the seniors wouldn't pass to the juniors and vice versa. The battles became so fierce that before long, the juniors and the seniors wouldn't even work together on the court during games. Our coach, Don Neff, had to platoon us. The seniors would start, and when a substitution became necessary, he'd put not one but five juniors in the game. We became two teams on one roster.

I don't remember exactly who started the rivalry that split our team, but I do remember that John Thomas and I embraced it early on. I've always been a leader, and I did my share of influencing other team members. Unfortunately, I have to confess that I led the juniors in the wrong direction.

What started as a bad attitude in one or two players made a mess of the situation for everyone. By the time we were in the thick of our schedule, even the players who didn't want to take part in the rivalry were affected. The season was a disaster. In the end, we finished with a mediocre record and never came close to reaching our potential. It just goes to show you, rotten attitudes ruin a team.

TALENT IS NOT ENOUGH

From my high school basketball experience I learned that talent is not enough to bring success to a team. Of course, you need talent. My friend Lou Holtz, the outstanding college football coach, observed, "You've got to have great athletes to win . . . You can't win without good athletes, but you can lose with them." But it also takes much more than talented people to win.

My high school teammates were loaded with talent, and if that were enough, we could have been state champions. But we were also loaded with rotten attitudes. You know which won the battle between talent and attitude in the end. Perhaps that is why to this day I understand the importance of a positive attitude and have placed such a strong emphasis on it for myself, for my children as they were growing up, and for the teams I lead.

Years ago I wrote something about attitude for my book *The Winning Attitude*. I'd like to share it with you:

> Attitude . . .
> It is the "advance man" of our true selves.
> Its roots are inward but its fruit is outward.
> It is our best friend or our worst enemy.
> It is more honest and more consistent than our words.
> It is an outward look based on past experiences.
> It is a thing which draws people to us or repels them.
> It is never content until it is expressed.
> It is the librarian of our past.
> It is the speaker of our present.
> It is the prophet of our future.[1]

Good attitudes among players do not guarantee a team's success, but bad attitudes guarantee its failure. The following five truths about attitudes clarify how they affect teamwork and a leader's team:

1. Attitudes Have the Power to Lift Up or Tear Down a Team

In *The Winner's Edge* Denis Waitley stated, "The real leaders in business, in the professional community, in education, in government, and in the home also seem to draw upon a special cutting edge that separates them from the rest of society. The winner's edge is not in a gifted birth, in a high IQ, or in talent. The winner's edge is in the attitude, not aptitude."[2]

Unfortunately, I think too many people resist that notion. They want to believe that talent alone (or talent with experience) is enough. But plenty of talented teams out there never amount to anything because of the attitudes of their players.

Various attitudes may impact a team made up of highly talented players:

Abilities	+	Attitudes	=	Result
Great Talent	+	Rotten Attitudes	=	Bad Team
Great Talent	+	Bad Attitudes	=	Average Team
Great Talent	+	Average Attitudes	=	Good Team
Great Talent	+	Good Attitudes	=	Great Team

If you want outstanding results, you need good people with great talent and awesome attitudes. When attitudes go up, so does the potential of the team. When attitudes go down, the potential of the team goes with it.

2. AN ATTITUDE COMPOUNDS WHEN EXPOSED TO OTHERS

Several things on a team are not contagious: talent, experience, and willingness to practice. But you can be sure of one thing: Attitude is catching. When someone on the team is teachable and his humility is rewarded by improvement, others are more likely to display similar characteristics. When a leader is upbeat in the face of discouraging circumstances, others admire that quality and want to be like her. When a team member displays a strong work ethic and begins to have a positive impact, others imitate him. People become inspired by their peers. People have a tendency to adopt the attitudes of those they spend time with—to pick up on their mind-sets, beliefs, and approaches to challenges.

The story of Roger Bannister is an inspiring example of the way attitudes often "compound." During the first half of the twentieth century, many sports experts believed that no runner could run a mile in less than four minutes. And for a long time they were right. But then on May 6, 1954, British runner and university student Roger Bannister ran a mile in 3 minutes 59.4 seconds during a meet in Oxford. Less than two months later, another runner, Australian John Landy, also broke the four-minute barrier. Then suddenly dozens and then hundreds of others broke it. Why? Because the best runners' attitudes changed. They began to adopt the mind-sets and beliefs of their peers.

Bannister's attitude and actions compounded when exposed to others. His attitude spread. Today, every world-class runner who competes at that distance can run a mile in less than four minutes. Attitudes are contagious!

3. Bad Attitudes Compound Faster Than Good Ones

There's only one thing more contagious than a good attitude—a bad attitude. For some reason many people think it's chic to be negative. I suspect that they think it makes them appear smart or important. But the truth is that a negative attitude hurts rather than helps the person who has it. And it also hurts the people around him.

To see how quickly and easily an attitude or mind-set can spread, just think about this story from Norman Cousins: Once during a football game, a doctor at the first aid station treated five people for what he suspected might be food poisoning. He soon discovered that all five people had bought drinks from a particular concession stand at the stadium.

The physician requested that the announcer advise people in the stadium to avoid buying drinks from the particular vendor because of the possibility of food poisoning. Before long, more than two hundred people complained of food poisoning symptoms. Nearly half the people's symptoms were so severe that they were taken to the hospital.

The story doesn't end there, however. After a little more

detective work, it was discovered that the five original victims had eaten tainted potato salad from one particular deli on the way to the game. When the other "sufferers" found out that the drinks in the stadium were safe, they experienced miraculous recoveries. That just goes to show you, an attitude spreads very quickly.

4. ATTITUDES ARE SUBJECTIVE, SO IDENTIFYING A WRONG ONE CAN BE DIFFICULT

Have you ever interacted with someone for the first time and suspected that his attitude was poor, yet you were unable to put your finger on exactly what was wrong? I believe many people have that experience.

ATTITUDE IS REALLY ABOUT HOW A PERSON IS.
THAT OVERFLOWS INTO HOW HE ACTS.

The reason people doubt their observations about others' attitudes is that attitudes are subjective. Someone with a bad attitude may not do anything illegal or unethical, yet his attitude may be ruining the team just the same.

People always project on the outside how they feel on the inside. Attitude is really about how a person is. That overflows into how he acts. Allow me to share with you common rotten attitudes that ruin a team so that you can recognize them for what they are when you see them.

An inability to admit wrongdoing. Have you ever spent time with people who never admit they're wrong? It's painful. Nobody's perfect, but someone who thinks he is does not make an ideal teammate. His wrong attitude will always create conflict.

Failing to forgive. It's said that Clara Barton, the founder of modern nursing, was once encouraged to bemoan a cruel act inflicted on her years earlier, but Barton wouldn't take the bait.

"Don't you remember the wrong that was done to you?" the friend goaded.

"No," answered Barton, "I distinctly remember forgetting that."

Holding a grudge is never positive or appropriate. And when unforgiveness occurs between teammates, it's certain to hurt the team.

Petty jealousy. An attitude that really works against people is the desire for equality that feeds petty jealousy. For some reason the people with this attitude believe that every person deserves equal treatment, regardless of talent, performance, or impact. Yet nothing could be farther from the truth. Each of us is created uniquely and performs differently, and as a result, we should be treated as such.

The disease of me. In his book *The Winner Within*, highly successful NBA coach Pat Riley writes about the "disease of me." He says of team members who have it, "They develop an overpowering belief in their own importance. Their actions virtually shout the claim, 'I'm the one.'" Riley asserts that the disease always has the same inevitable result: "The Defeat of Us."[3]

A critical spirit. Fred and Martha were driving home after a church service. "Fred," Martha asked, "did you notice that the pastor's sermon was kind of weak today?"

"No, not really," answered Fred.

"Well, did you hear that the choir was flat?"

"No, I didn't," he responded.

"Well, you certainly must have noticed that young couple and their children right in front of us, with all the noise and commotion they made the whole service!"

"I'm sorry, dear, but no, I didn't."

Finally in disgust Martha said, "Honestly, Fred, I don't know why you even bother to go to church."

When someone on the team has a critical spirit, everybody knows it because everyone on the team can do no right.

A desire to hog all the credit. Another bad attitude that hurts the team is similar to the "disease of me." But where the person with that disease may simmer in the background and create dissension, the credit hog continually steps into the spotlight to take a bow—whether he has earned it or not. His attitude is opposite that of NBA Hall of Fame center Bill

Russell, who said of his time on the court, "The most important measure of how good a game I played was how much better I'd made my teammates play."

Certainly there are other negative attitudes that I haven't named, but my intention isn't to list every bad attitude—just some of the most common ones. In a word, most bad attitudes are the result of selfishness. If one of your teammates puts others down, sabotages teamwork, or makes himself out to be more important than the team, then you can be sure that you've encountered someone with a bad attitude.

5. Rotten Attitudes, Left Alone, Ruin Everything

Bad attitudes must be addressed. You can be sure that they will always cause dissension, resentment, combativeness, and division on a team. And they will never go away on their own if they are left unaddressed. They will simply fester and ruin a team—along with its chances of reaching its potential.

Because people with bad attitudes are so difficult to deal with and because attitudes seem so subjective, you may doubt your gut reaction when you encounter someone with a bad attitude. After all, if it's only your opinion that he has a rotten attitude, then you have no right to address it, right? Not if you care about the team. Rotten attitudes ruin a team. That is always true. If you leave a bad apple in a barrel of good apples, you will always end up with a barrel of rotten apples. Attitudes always impact a leader's effectiveness.

President Thomas Jefferson remarked, "Nothing can stop the man with the right mental attitude from achieving his goal; nothing on earth can help the man with the wrong mental attitude." If you care about your team and you are committed to helping all of the players, you can't ignore a bad attitude.

Dealing with a person whose attitude is bad can be a very tricky thing. Before you try to address the issue, you would benefit from a closer look at attitudes and how they affect an individual.

2

How Does Attitude Impact an Individual?

Your attitude and your potential go hand in hand.

What is attitude? How do you put your finger on it? Well, attitude is an inward feeling expressed by behavior. That is why an attitude can be seen without a word being said. Haven't we all noticed "the pout" of the sulker, or the "jutted jaw" of the determined? Of all the things we wear, our expression is the most important.

Sometimes our attitude can be masked outwardly and others who see us are fooled. But usually the cover-ups will not last long. There is that constant struggle as the attitude tries to wiggle its way out.

My father enjoys telling the story of the four-year-old who had one of those trouble-filled days. After reprimanding him, his mother finally said to him, "Son, you go over to that chair and sit on it now!" The little lad went to the chair, sat down and said, "Mommy, I'm sitting on the outside, but I'm standing up on the inside."

Psychologist/philosopher James Allen states, "A person cannot travel within and stand still without." Soon what is happening within us will affect what is happening without. A hardened attitude is a dreaded disease. It causes a closed mind and a dark future. When our attitude is positive and conducive to growth, the mind expands and the progress begins.

ATTITUDE DETERMINES SUCCESS OR FAILURE

While leading a conference in South Carolina, I tried the following experiment. I asked the audience, "What word describes what will determine our happiness, acceptance, peace, and success?" The audience began to express words such as *job, education, money, time.* Finally someone said *attitude.* Such an important area of their lives was a second thought. Our attitude is the primary force that will determine whether we succeed or fail.

For some, attitude presents a difficulty in every opportunity; for others it presents an opportunity in every difficulty. Some climb with a positive attitude, while others fall with a negative perspective. The very fact that the attitude "makes some" while "breaking others" is significant enough for us to explore its importance. Here are seven axioms about attitude to help you better understand how it impacts a person's life:

Attitude Axiom #1: Our Attitude Determines Our Approach to Life

Our attitude tells us what we expect from life. Like an airplane, if our "nose" is pointed up, we are taking off; if it is pointed down, we may be headed for a crash.

One of my favorite stories is about a grandpa and grandma who visited their grandchildren. Each afternoon Grandpa would lie down for a nap. One day, as a practical joke, the kids decided to put Limburger cheese in his mustache. Quite soon he awoke sniffing. "Why, this room stinks," he exclaimed as he got up and went out into the kitchen. He wasn't there long until he decided that the kitchen smelled too, so he walked outdoors for a breath of fresh air. Much to Grandpa's surprise, the open air brought no relief, and he proclaimed, "The whole world stinks!"

How true that is to life! When we carry "Limburger cheese" in our attitudes, the whole world smells bad. We are individually responsible for our view of life. That truth has been known for ages and is contained in Scripture: "For whatever a man sows, that he will also reap."[1] Our attitude toward and action in life help determine what happens to us.

It would be impossible to estimate the number of jobs lost, the number of promotions missed, the number of sales not made, and the number of marriages ruined by poor attitudes.

But almost daily we witness jobs that are held but hated and marriages that are tolerated but unhappy, all because people are waiting for others, or the world, to change instead of realizing that they are responsible for their own behavior.

ATTITUDE AXIOM #2: OUR ATTITUDE DETERMINES OUR RELATIONSHIPS WITH PEOPLE

All of life is impacted by your relationships with people, yet establishing relationships is difficult. You can't get along with some people, and you can't make it without them. That's why it is essential to build proper relationships with others in our crowded world.

The Stanford Research Institute says that the money you make in any endeavor is determined only 12.5 percent by knowledge and 87.5 percent by your ability to deal with people.

87.5% people knowledge   +   12.5% product knowledge   =   Success

That is why Teddy Roosevelt said, "The most important single ingredient to the formula of success is knowing how to get along with people." And why John D. Rockefeller said, "I will pay more for the ability to deal with people than any other ability under the sun."

When the attitude we possess places others first and we see people as important, then our perspective will reflect their viewpoint, not ours. Until we walk in the other person's shoes and see life through another's eyes, we will be like the man who angrily jumped out of his car after a collision with another car. "Why don't you people watch where you're driving?" he shouted wildly. "You're the fourth car I've hit today!"

Usually the person who rises within an organization has a good attitude. The promotions did not give that individual an outstanding attitude, but an outstanding attitude resulted in promotions.

Attitude Axiom #3: Often Our Attitude Is the Only Difference Between Success and Failure

History's greatest achievements have been made by men who excelled only slightly over the masses of others in their fields. This could be called the principle of the slight edge. Many times that slight difference was attitude. The former Israeli Prime Minister Golda Meir underlined this truth in one of her interviews. She said, "All my country has is spirit. We don't have petroleum dollars. We don't have mines of great wealth in the ground. We don't have the support of a worldwide public opinion that looks favorably on us. All Israel has is the spirit of its people. And if the people lose their spirit, even the United States of America cannot save us."

Certainly aptitude is important to our success in life. Yet success or failure in any undertaking is caused more by mental attitude than by mere mental capacities. I remember times when Margaret, my wife, would come home from teaching school frustrated because of modern education's emphasis on aptitude instead of attitude. She wanted the kids to be tested on A.Q. (attitude quotient) instead of just the I.Q. (intelligence quotient). She would talk of kids whose I.Q. was high yet their performance was low. There were others whose I.Q. was low but their performance was high.

As a parent, I hope my children have excellent minds and outstanding attitudes. But if I had to choose an "either-or" situation, without hesitation I would want their A.Q. to be high.

A Yale University president some years ago gave similar advice to a former president of Ohio State: "Always be kind to your A and B students. Someday one of them will return to your campus as a good professor. And also be kind to your C students. Someday one of them will return and build a two-million-dollar science laboratory."

There is very little difference in people, but that little difference makes a big difference. The little difference is attitude. The big difference is whether it is positive or negative.

Attitude Axiom #4: Our Attitude at the Beginning of a Task Will Affect Its Outcome More Than Anything Else

Coaches understand the importance of their teams' having the right attitude before facing a tough opponent. Surgeons want to see their patients mentally prepared before going into surgery. Job-seekers know that their prospective employer is looking for more than just skills when they apply for work. Public speakers want a conducive atmosphere before they communicate to their audience. Why? Because the right attitude in the beginning ensures success at the end. You are acquainted with the saying "All's well that ends well." An equal truth is "All's well that begins well."

Most projects fail or succeed before they begin. A young mountain climber and an experienced guide were ascending a high peak in the Sierras. Early one morning the young climber was suddenly awakened by a tremendous cracking sound. He was convinced that the end of the world had come. The guide responded, "It's not the end of the world, just the dawning of a new day." As the sun rose, it was merely hitting the ice and causing it to melt.

Many times we have been guilty of viewing our future challenges as the sunset of life rather than the sunrise of a bright new opportunity.

For instance, there's the story of two shoe salesmen who were sent to an island to sell shoes. The first salesman, upon arrival, was shocked to realize that no one wore shoes. Immediately he sent a telegram to his home office in Chicago saying, "Will return home tomorrow. No one wears shoes."

The second salesman was thrilled by the same realization. Immediately he wired the home office in Chicago saying, "Please send me 10,000 shoes. Everyone here needs them."

ATTITUDE AXIOM #5: OUR ATTITUDE CAN TURN OUR PROBLEMS INTO BLESSINGS

In *Awake, My Heart,* J. Sidlow Baxter wrote, "What is the difference between an obstacle and an opportunity? Our attitude toward it. Every opportunity has a difficulty and every difficulty has an opportunity."[2]

When confronted with a difficult situation, a person with an outstanding attitude makes the best of it while he gets the worst of it. Life can be likened to a grindstone. Whether it grinds you down or polishes you depends upon what you are made of.

While attending a conference of young leaders, I heard this statement: "No society has ever developed tough men during times of peace." Adversity is prosperity to those who possess a great attitude. Kites rise against, not with, the wind. When the adverse wind of criticism blows, allow it to be to you what the blast of wind is to the kite—a force against it that lifts it higher. A kite would not fly unless it had the controlling tension of the string to tie it down. It is equally true in life. Consider the following successes that were accomplished through a positive attitude.

WHEN CONFRONTED WITH A DIFFICULT SITUATION,
A PERSON WITH AN OUTSTANDING ATTITUDE MAKES THE
BEST OF IT WHILE HE GETS THE WORST OF IT.

When Napoleon's school companions made sport of him because of his humble origin and poverty, he devoted himself entirely to his books. Quickly rising above his classmates in scholarship, he commanded their respect. Soon he was regarded as the brightest in the class.

Few people knew Abraham Lincoln until the great weight of the Civil War showed his character.

Robinson Crusoe was written in prison. John Bunyan wrote *Pilgrim's Progress* in the Bedford jail. Sir Walter Raleigh wrote *The History of the World* during a thirteen-year imprisonment. Luther translated the Bible while confined in the castle of Wartburg. For ten years Dante, author of *The Divine Comedy*, worked in exile and under the sentence of death. Beethoven was almost totally deaf and burdened with sorrow when he produced his greatest works.

When God wants to educate someone, He does not send

him to the school of graces but to the school of necessities. Great leaders emerge when crises occur. In the lives of people who achieve, we read repeatedly of terrible troubles that forced them to rise above the commonplace. Not only do they find the answers, but they also discover a tremendous power within themselves. Like a groundswell far out in the ocean, this force within explodes into a mighty wave when circumstances seem to overcome. Then out steps the athlete, the author, the statesman, the scientist, or the businessman. David Sarnoff said, "There is plenty of security in the cemetery; I long for opportunity."

ATTITUDE AXIOM #6: OUR ATTITUDE CAN GIVE US AN UNCOMMONLY POSITIVE PERSPECTIVE

An uncommonly positive perspective is able to help us accomplish some uncommon goals. I have keenly observed the different approaches and results achieved by a positive thinker and by a person filled with fear and apprehension. For example, in ancient Israel when Goliath came up against the Hebrews, the soldiers all thought, *He's so big we can never kill him.* David looked at the same giant and thought, *He's so big I can't miss.*

George Sweeting, former president of Moody Bible Institute, tells a story about a Scotsman who was an extremely hard worker and expected all the men under him to be the same. His men would tease him, "Scotty, don't you know that Rome wasn't built in a day?" "Yes," he would answer, "I know that. But I wasn't foreman on that job."

Individuals whose attitudes cause them to approach life from an entirely positive perspective are not always understood. They are what some would call a "no-limit people." In other words, they don't accept the normal limitations of life as most people do. They are unwilling to accept "the accepted" just because it is accepted. Their response to self-limiting conditions will probably be "why?" instead of "okay." Certainly, they have limitations. Their gifts are not so plentiful that they cannot fail. But they are determined to walk to the very edge of their potential and the potential of their goals before accepting defeat.

They are like bumblebees. According to a theory of aerodynamics, as demonstrated through the wind tunnel tests, the bumblebee should be unable to fly. Because of the size, weight, and shape of its body in relationship to the total wing span, flying is scientifically impossible. The bumblebee, being ignorant of scientific theory, goes ahead and flies anyway and makes honey every day.

The future not only looks bright when the attitude is right, but also the present is much more enjoyable. The positive person understands that the journey of success is as enjoyable as the destination. Asked which of his works he would select as his masterpiece, architect Frank Lloyd Wright, at the age of eighty-three, replied, "My next one."

A friend of mine in Ohio drove eighteen-wheelers for an interstate trucking company. Knowing the hundreds of miles he logged weekly, I once asked him how he kept from getting extremely tired. "It's all in your attitude," he replied. "Some drivers 'go to work' in the morning, but I 'go for a ride in the country.'" That kind of positive perspective gives him the "edge" on life.

ATTITUDE AXIOM #7: YOUR ATTITUDE IS NOT AUTOMATICALLY GOOD BECAUSE YOU ARE A RELIGIOUS PERSON

It is noteworthy that the seven deadly sins—pride, covetousness, lust, envy, anger, gluttony, and sloth—are all matters of attitude, inner spirit, and motives. Sadly, many people of faith carry with them inner-spirit problems. They are like the elder brother contained in the parable of the prodigal son, thinking that they do everything right. While the younger brother left home to live a wild life, the elder brother chose to stay home with his father. He wasn't going to spend *his* time sowing wild oats! Yet, when the younger brother returned home, some of the elder brother's wrong attitudes began to surface.

First was a feeling of self-importance. The elder brother

was out in the field doing what he ought to do, but he got mad when the party began at home—his father would never let him have one for himself!

That was followed by a feeling of self-pity. The elder brother said, "Look! For so many years I have been serving you, and you have never thrown a party for me. But when your son who wasted all of your money comes home, you give him a big celebration."[3]

Often people overlook the true meaning of the story of the prodigal son. They forget that there are not one but two prodigals. The younger brother is guilty of the sins of the flesh, whereas the elder brother is guilty of the sins of the spirit. His problem is his attitude. At the end of the parable, it is the elder brother—the second prodigal—who is outside the father's house.

And that is a good lesson for all of us to remember. A poor attitude will take us places we don't want to go. Sometimes it can even take you completely out of the game. On the other hand, a good attitude puts you in the place of greatest potential.

Perhaps you're not sure if your attitude is where it ought to be. Or maybe you are leading someone whose attitude isn't as positive as it could be. How do you address that? First, you need to know how a person's attitude is formed. That's the subject of the next chapter.

PART II

THE FORMATION OF ATTITUDE

WHAT SHAPES A PERSON'S ATTITUDE?

A lot goes into an attitude—but a lot more comes out of it!

Attitudes aren't shaped in a vacuum. People are born with certain characteristics, and those impact their attitudes. But many other factors play an even greater role in people's lives and in the formation of their attitudes. While these factors continually impact people, in general, they make the greatest impression during the following times of life:

STAGES	FACTORS
PRE-BIRTH:	Inherent personality/temperament
BIRTH:	Environment
AGES 1–6:	Word expression
	Adult acceptance/affirmation
AGES 6–10:	Self-image
	Exposure to new experiences
AGES 11–21:	Peers, physical appearance
AGES 21–61:	Marriage, family, job, success
	Adjustments, assessment of life

PERSONALITY—WHO I AM

All people are born as distinct individuals. Even two children with the same parents, same environment, and same training are totally different from each other. These differences contribute to the "spice of life" we all enjoy. Like tract homes that all look alike, if we all had similar personalities, our journey through life would certainly be boring.

GENERALLY, PEOPLE WITH CERTAIN TEMPERAMENTS DEVELOP SPECIFIC ATTITUDES COMMON TO THAT TEMPERAMENT.

I love the story of two men out fishing together who began discussing their wives. One said, "If all men were like me, they would all want to be married to my wife." The other man quickly replied, "If they were all like me, none of them would want to be married to her."

A set of attitudes accompanies each personality type. Generally, people with certain temperaments develop specific attitudes common to that temperament. A few years ago, Tim LaHaye, co-author of the popular "Left Behind" novels, lectured and wrote about the four basic temperaments. Through observation, I have noticed that a person with what he calls a *choleric* personality often exhibits attitudes of perseverance and aggressiveness. A *sanguine* person is generally positive and looks on the bright side of life. An introspective *melancholy* individual can be negative at times, while a *phlegmatic* is prone to say, "Easy come, easy go." Every individual's personality is composed of a mixture of these temperaments, and there are exceptions to these generalizations. However, a temperament ordinarily follows a track that can be identified by tracing a person's attitudes.

ENVIRONMENT—WHAT'S AROUND ME

I believe that environment is a greater controlling factor in our attitude development than our personality or other inherited traits. Before my wife, Margaret, and I began our family we decided to adopt our children. We wanted to give a child who might not normally have the benefit of a loving faith-filled home an opportunity to live in that environment. Although our children may not physically resemble us, they certainly have been molded by the environment in which we have reared them.

The environment of early childhood develops a person's "belief system." Children continually pick up priorities, attitudes, interests, and philosophies from their environment. It is a fact that what I really believe affects my attitude! However, the things I believe may not be true. What I believe may not be healthy. It may even hurt others and destroy me. Yet an attitude is reinforced by a belief—whether it is right or wrong.

Environment is the first influencer of our belief system. Therefore the foundation of an attitude is laid in the environment to which we were born. Environment becomes even more significant when we realize that the beginning attitudes are the most difficult to change.

WORD EXPRESSION—WHAT I HEAR

You've undoubtedly heard the old saying: "Sticks and stones may break my bones, but names will never hurt me." Don't you believe that! In fact, after the bruises have disappeared and the physical pain is gone, the inward pain of hurtful words remains.

Years ago when I was leading a church, during one of our staff meetings I asked the pastors, secretaries, and custodians to raise their hands if they could remember a childhood experience that hurt deeply because of someone's words. Everyone raised his hand. One pastor recalled the time when he sat in a reading circle at school. (Do you remember how intimidating those sessions were?) When his time came to read, he mispronounced the word *photography*. He read it photo-graphy instead of pho-tog-ra-phy. The teacher corrected him and the class laughed. He still remembers . . . forty years later. One positive result of that experience was his desire from that moment on to pronounce words correctly.

Today one of the reasons he excels as a speaker is be-cause of that determination.

ADULT ACCEPTANCE/AFFIRMATION—
WHAT I FEEL

Often when I am speaking to leaders, I tell them about the importance of accepting and affirming the ones they are lead-ing. The truth is, people don't care how much you know until they know how much you care!

Think back to your school days. Who was your favorite teacher? Now think of why. Probably your warmest memo-ries are of someone who accepted and affirmed you. We sel-dom remember what our teacher said to us, but we do remember how they loved us. Long before we understand teaching, we reach out for understanding. Long after we have forgotten the teachings, we remember the feeling of acceptance or rejection.

PEOPLE DON'T CARE HOW MUCH YOU KNOW
UNTIL THEY KNOW HOW MUCH YOU CARE.

Many times I have asked people if they enjoyed their pas-tor's sermon the previous week. After a positive response I ask, "What was his subject?" Seventy-five percent of the time they cannot give me the sermon title. They do not remember the exact subject, but they do remember the atmosphere and attitude in which it was delivered.

My favorite Sunday school teachers from my childhood are beautiful examples of this truth. First came Katie, my second grade teacher. When I was sick and missed her class, she would come and visit me on Monday. She would ask how I was feeling and give me a five-cent trinket that was worth a million dollars to me. Katie would say, "Johnny, I always teach better when you are in the class. When you come next Sunday morning, would you raise your hand so I can see you are in attendance? Then I will teach better."

I can still remember raising my hand and watching Katie smile at me from the front of the class. I also remember other kids raising their hands on Sundays when Katie began to teach and her class grew rapidly. That year, the Sunday school superintendent wanted to split the class and start a new one across the hall. He asked for volunteers for the new class and no one raised his hand. Why? No kid wanted to go with a new teacher and miss Katie's continual demonstration of love.

Another teacher I remember is Glen Leatherwood. He taught all the junior high school boys in the church where I grew up. Did you ever teach a group of ten-wiggles-per-minute boys? Usually those teachers go straight from teaching that class to their heavenly reward! But not Glen. He taught junior high boys for another thirty years. The twelve months I spent in his class made a profound impact on my faith and my life's work.

I was also privileged to grow up in a very affirming family. I never questioned my parents' love and acceptance. They continually affirmed their love through actions and words. When our children were growing up, Margaret and I tried to create that same environment for them. I believe that our kids saw or sensed our acceptance and affirmation at least thirty times a day. Today I'd say our grandchildren get almost twice as much. That's not too much! Have you ever been told too many times that you are important, loved, and appreciated? Remember, people don't care how much you know until they know how much you care.

SELF-IMAGE—HOW I SEE MYSELF

It is impossible to perform consistently in a manner inconsistent with the way we see ourselves. In other words, we usually act in direct response to our self-image. Nothing is more difficult to accomplish than changing outward actions without changing inward feelings.

One of the best ways to improve those inward feelings is to put some "success" under your belt. My daughter Elizabeth has a tendency to be shy and wants to hold back on new experiences. But once she has warmed up to a situation, it's "full steam ahead." When she was in first grade, her school had a candy bar sale. Each child was given thirty candy bars and was challenged to sell every one of them. When I picked up Elizabeth from school she was holding her "challenge" and needed some positive encouragement. It was time for a sales meeting with my new salesgirl.

All the way home I taught her how to sell candy bars. I surrounded each teaching point with a half dozen "You can do it—your smile will win them over—I believe in you" phrases. By the end of our fifteen-minute drive, the young lady sitting beside me had become a charming, committed saleslady. Off she went to the neighborhood with little brother Joel eating one of the candy bars and declaring that it was truly the best he had ever devoured.

At the end of the day, all thirty bars had been sold and Elizabeth was feeling great. I will never forget the words she prayed as I tucked her into bed that night: "O God, thanks for the candy sale at school. It's great. O Lord, help make me a winner! Amen."

Elizabeth's prayer reflects the heart's desire of every person. We all want to be winners. Sure enough, Elizabeth came home the next day with another box of candy bars. Now the big test! She'd exhausted the supply of friendly neighbors, and she was thrust into the cruel world of the unknown buyer.

Elizabeth admitted fear as we went to a shopping center to sell our wares. Again I offered encouragement, a few more selling tips, more encouragement, the right location, more encouragement. And she did it. The experience amounted to two days of selling, two sold-out performances, two happy people, and one boosted self-image.

How we see ourselves reflects how others see us. If we like ourselves, it increases the odds that others will like us. Self-image sets the parameters for the construction of our attitudes. We act in response to how we see ourselves. We will never go beyond the boundaries that stake out our true feelings about ourselves. Those "new territories" can be explored only when our self-image is strong enough to give us permission to go there.

EXPOSURE TO NEW EXPERIENCES— OPPORTUNITIES FOR GROWTH

French philosopher François Voltaire likened life to a game of cards. Each player must accept the cards dealt to him. But once those cards are in the hand, he alone decides how to play them to win the game.

We always have a number of opportunities in our hand, and we must decide whether to take a risk and act on them. Nothing in life causes more stress, yet at the same time provides more opportunity for growth, than new experiences.

If you are a parent, you will find it impossible to shield your children from new experiences that might be negative. So it is essential to prepare positive encounters that will build self-image and confidence. Both positive and negative experiences can be used as tools in preparing children for life.

Children need continual reassurance and praise when their new experiences are less than positive. In fact, the worse the experience, the more encouragement they need. But sometimes we become discouraged when they are discouraged. This is a good formula to adopt:

New experiences + teaching applications x love = growth.

ASSOCIATION WITH PEERS— WHO INFLUENCES ME

What others indicate about their perceptions of us affects how we perceive ourselves. Usually we respond to the expectations of others. This truth becomes evident to parents when their children go to school. No longer can parents control their children's environment.

My parents understood that others could exercise a sizable amount of control over their sons' behavior, so they were determined to watch and control our peer relation-ships as much as possible. Their strategy: Provide a climate in the Maxwell home that was appealing to their two boys' friends. This meant sacrificing their finances and time. They provided us with a shuffleboard game, Ping-Pong table, pool table, pinball machine, chemistry set, basketball court, and all the sports equipment imaginable. We also had a mother who was spectator, referee, counselor, arbitrator, and fan.

And the kids came, often twenty to twenty-five at a time. All sizes, shapes, and colors. Everyone had fun and my parents observed our friends. Sometimes, after the gang had gone, my parents would ask about one of our friends. They would openly discuss his language or atti-tudes and encourage us not to act or think that way. I real-ize now that most of my major decisions as a young boy were influenced by my parents' teaching and observation of my associations.

Casey Stengel, who was a successful manager of the New York Yankees baseball team, understood the power of associ-ations on a ballplayer's attitude. He gave Billy Martin some advice when he was a rookie manager. Martin recalled, "Casey said there would be fifteen players on your team who will run through a wall for you, five who will hate you, and five who are undecided. When you make out your rooming list, always room your losers together. Never room a good guy with a loser. Those losers who stay together will blame the manager for everything, but it won't spread if you keep them isolated."

Charles "Tremendous" Jones, author of *Life Is Tremendous*, says, "What you will become in five years will be determined by what you read and who you associate with." That's good for all of us to remember.

PHYSICAL APPEARANCE—
HOW WE LOOK TO OTHERS

Our looks play an important part in the construction of our attitude. Incredible pressure is placed upon people to possess the "in look," which seems to be the standard of acceptance. The next time you're watching television, notice how much the commercials emphasize looks. Notice the percentage of ads dealing with clothing, diet, exercise, and overall physical attractiveness. Hollywood says, "Blandness is out and beauty is in." This influences our perception of our worth.

What can make it even more difficult is the realization that others also judge our worth by our appearance. Recently, I read a business article that stated, "Our physical attractiveness helps determine our income." For example, the research reported in that article showed the discrepancies between the salaries of men 6'2" and 5'10". The taller men consistently received higher salaries. Like it or not, physical appearance (and one's perception of it) impacts a person's attitude.

MARRIAGE, FAMILY, AND JOB— OUR SECURITY AND STATUS

New influences begin to affect our attitude as we approach our mid-twenties. It is during this time that most people start a career. They also often get married. That means another person influences our perspective.

When I speak on attitudes, I always emphasize the need to surround ourselves with positive people. One of the saddest comments that I often receive comes from someone who tells me their marriage partner is negative and doesn't want to change. To a certain extent, when the negative mate does not want to change, the positive one is imprisoned by negativism. In such situations I advise the couple to remember their spouse as the person they loved in their courtship days. Their marriage will improve if each other's weaknesses are not emphasized. But many end up in divorce court because the strengths are ignored. The partners go from expecting the best to expecting the worst, from building on strengths to focusing on weaknesses.

All of the factors I've mentioned go into the "mix" of attitude. They have impacted who you are and those whom you lead. But remember this: Whether you are eleven, forty-two, or sixty-five, your attitude toward life is *still* under construction. It's never too late for a person to change his attitude. And that's the subject of the next chapter.

4

CAN AN ATTITUDE BE CHANGED?

The key to having a good attitude
is the willingness to change.

We are either the masters or the victims of our attitudes. It is a matter of personal choice. Who we are today is the result of choices we made yesterday. Tomorrow we will become what we choose today. To change means to choose to change.

I'm told that in northern Canada there are just two seasons: winter and July. When the back roads begin to thaw, they become muddy. Vehicles going into the backwoods country leave deep ruts that become frozen when cold weather returns. For those entering remote areas during the winter months, there are signs that read, "Driver, please choose carefully which rut you drive in, because you'll be in it for the next twenty miles."

Some people seem to feel stuck in their current attitudes, like a car in a twenty-mile rut. However, attitude is not permanent. If you're not happy with yours, know that you can change it. If someone you lead has a bad attitude, then you can help them to change—but only if they truly *want* to change. Anyone can become the kind of positive person for whom life is a joy and every day is filled with potential if they genuinely desire to.

If you want to have a great attitude, then make the following choices:

CHOICE #1: EVALUATE YOUR PRESENT ATTITUDE

The process begins with knowing where you're starting from. Evaluating your present attitude will take some time. If possible, try to separate yourself from your attitude. The goal of this exercise is not to see the "bad you" but a "bad attitude" that keeps you from being a more fulfilled person. You can make key changes only when you identify the problem.

When he sees a logjam, the professional logger climbs a tall tree and locates a key log, blows that log free, and lets the stream do the rest. An amateur would start at the edge of the jam and move all the logs, eventually moving the key log. Obviously, both methods will get the logs moving, but the professional does his work more quickly and effectively.

To find the key "logs" in your attitude, use the following evaluation process (and write your answers in a journal or someplace where you can later refer back to them):

Identify Problem Feelings: What attitudes make you feel the most negative about yourself? Usually feelings can be sensed before the problem is clarified.

Identify Problem Behavior: What attitudes cause you the most problems when dealing with others?

Identify Problem Thinking: We are the sum of our thoughts. "As a man thinks within himself, so he is."[1] What thoughts consistently control your mind? Although this is the beginning step in correcting attitude problems, these are not as easy to identify as the first two.

Clarify Truth: In order to know how to change, you need to examine your feelings in light of truth. If you are a person of faith, then use the Scriptures. What do they tell you about how your attitude should be?

Secure Commitment: At this stage, "What must I do to change?" turns into "I must change." Remember, the choice to change is the one decision that must be made, and only you can make it.

Plan and Carry Out Your Choice: Act on your decision immediately and repeatedly.

CHOICE #2: REALIZE THAT FAITH IS STRONGER THAN FEAR

The only thing that will guarantee the success of a difficult or doubtful undertaking is faith from the beginning that you can do it. Philosopher William James said, "The greatest discovery of my generation is that people can alter their lives by altering their attitudes of mind." Change depends on your frame of mind. Believe that you can change. Ask your friends and colleagues to encourage you at every opportunity. And if you are a person of faith, ask for God's help. He knows your problems, and He is willing and able to help you overcome them.

CHOICE #3: WRITE A STATEMENT OF PURPOSE

When I was a boy, my father decided to build a basketball court for my brother and me. He made a cement driveway, put a backboard on the garage and was just getting ready to put up the basket when he was called away on an emergency. He promised to put up the hoop as soon as he returned. *No problem*, I thought. *I have a brand-new Spalding ball and a new cement driveway on which to dribble it.* For a few minutes I bounced the ball on the cement. Soon that became boring, so I took the ball and threw it up against the backboard—once. I let the ball run off the court and didn't pick it up again until Dad returned to put up the rim. Why? It's no fun playing basketball without a goal. The joy is in having something to aim for.

In order to have fun and direction in changing your attitude, you must establish a clearly stated goal. This goal should be as specific as possible, written out and signed, with a time frame attached to it. The purpose statement should be placed in a visible spot where you see it several times a day to give you reinforcement.

You will attain this goal if each day you do three things:

1. WRITE SPECIFICALLY WHAT YOU DESIRE TO ACCOMPLISH EACH DAY.

The biblical story of David's encounter with Goliath is a fine illustration of faith and how it may overcome insurmountable odds with seemingly inadequate resources. But one thing perplexed me when I first began to study David's life. Why did he pick five stones for his sling on his way to encounter Goliath? The longer I pondered, the more perplexed I became. Why five stones? There was only one giant. Choosing five stones seemed to be a flaw in his faith. Did he think he was going to miss and that he would have four more chances? Some time later I was reading in 2 Samuel, and I got the answer. Goliath had four sons, so that means there were five giants. In David's reckoning, there was one stone per giant! Now that is what I mean about being specific in our faith.

What are the giants you must slay to make your attitude what it needs to be? What resources will you need? Don't be overcome with frustration when you see the problems. Take one giant at a time. Military strategists teach their armies to fight one front at a time. Settle which attitude you want to tackle at this time. Write it down. As you successfully begin to win battles, write them down. And spend time reading about past victories because it will encourage you.

2. VERBALIZE TO AN ENCOURAGING FRIEND WHAT YOU WANT TO ACCOMPLISH EACH DAY.

Belief is inward conviction; faith is outward action. You will receive both encouragement and accountability by verbalizing your intentions. One of the ways people resolve a conflict is to verbalize it to themselves or someone else. This practice is also vital in reaching your desired attitudes.

I know successful salesmen who repeat this phrase out loud fifty times each morning and fifty times each evening: "I can do it." Continually saying positive statements helps them believe in themselves and causes them to act on that belief. Start this process by changing your vocabulary. Here are some suggestions:

ELIMINATE THESE WORDS COMPLETELY	MAKE THESE WORDS A PART OF YOUR VOCABULARY
1. I can't	1. I can
2. If	2. I will

3. Doubt	3. Expect the best
4. I don't think	4. I know
5. I don't have the time	5. I will make the time
6. Maybe	6. Positively
7. I'm afraid of	7. I am confident
8. I don't believe	8. I do believe
9. (minimize) I	9. (promote) You
10. It's impossible	10. All things are possible

3. TAKE ACTION ON YOUR GOAL EACH DAY.

The difference between a wise man and a foolish one is his response to what he already knows: A wise man follows up on what he hears while a foolish man knows but does not act. To change, you must take action. And while you're at it, do something positive for someone else too. Nothing improves a person's outlook like unselfish service to someone with a greater need than their own.

CHOICE #4: HAVE THE DESIRE TO CHANGE

No choice will determine the success of your attitude change more than desiring to change. When all else fails, desire alone can keep you heading in the right direction. Many people have climbed over insurmountable obstacles to make themselves better when they realized that change is possible if they want it badly enough. Let me illustrate.

While hopping about one day, a frog happened to slip into a very large pothole along a country road. All of his attempts at jumping out were in vain. Soon a rabbit came upon the frog trapped in the hole and offered to help him out. He, too, failed. After various animals from the forest made three or four gallant attempts to help the poor frog out, they finally gave up. "We'll go back and get you some food," they said. "It looks like you're going to be here a while." However, not long after they took off to get food, they heard the frog hopping along after them. They couldn't believe it! "We thought you couldn't get out!" they exclaimed. "Oh, I couldn't," replied the frog. "But you see, there was a big truck coming right at me, and I had to."

FALL IN LOVE WITH THE CHALLENGE OF CHANGE AND WATCH THE DESIRE TO CHANGE GROW.

It is when we "have to get out of the potholes of life" that we change. As long as we have acceptable options, we will not change. The truth is that most people are more comfortable with old problems than new solutions. They respond to their needs for a turnaround in life like the Duke of Cambridge, who once said, "Any change, at any time, for any reason, is to be deplored." People who believe that nothing should ever be done for the first time never see anything done.

People can change, and that is the greatest motivation of all. Nothing sparks the fires of desire more than the sudden realization that you do not have to stay the same. Fall in love with the challenge of change and watch the desire to change grow. That's what happened to Aleida Huissen, seventy-eight, of Rotterdam, Netherlands. She had been a smoker for fifty years, and for fifty years she tried to give up the habit. But she was unsuccessful. Then Leo Jensen, seventy-nine, proposed marriage and refused to go through with the wedding until Aleida gave up smoking. Aleida says, "Willpower never was enough to get me off the habit. Love did it."

My life is dedicated to helping others reach their potential. I suggest that you follow the advice of Mark Twain, who said, "Take your mind out every now and then and dance on it. It is getting all caked up." It was his way of saying, "Get out of that rut." Too many times we settle into a set way of thinking and accept limitations that need not be placed upon us. Embrace change, and it will change you.

CHOICE #5: LIVE ONE DAY AT A TIME

Any person can fight the battle for just one day. It is only when you and I add the burdens of those two awful eternities, yesterday and tomorrow, that we tremble. It is not the experiences of today that drive people to distraction; it is the remorse or bitterness for something that happened yesterday and the dread of what tomorrow may bring. Let us therefore live but one day at a time—today!

CHOICE #6: CHANGE YOUR THOUGHT PATTERNS

That which holds our attention determines our actions. We are where we are and what we are because of the dominating thoughts that occupy our minds. Take a look at this syllogism. It emphasizes the power of our thought life:

Major premise: We can control our thoughts.
Minor premise: Our feelings come from our thoughts.
Conclusion: We can control our feelings by learning to change how we think.

It is that simple. Our feelings come from our thoughts. Therefore, we can change them by changing our thought patterns.

Our thought life, not our circumstances, determines our happiness. Often I see people who are convinced that they will be happy when they attain a certain goal. When they reach the goal, many times they do not find the fulfillment they anticipated. The secret to staying on an even keel? Fill your mind with good thoughts. The apostle Paul advised, "Whatever things are true, whatever things are noble . . . whatever things are of good report, if there is any virtue and if there is anything praiseworthy—meditate on these things."[2] He understood that the things that hold our attention determine our action.

CHOICE #7: DEVELOP GOOD HABITS

An attitude is nothing more than a habit of thought. The process for developing habits—good or bad—is the same. It is as easy to form the habit of succeeding as it is to succumb to the habit of failure.

Habits aren't instincts; they're acquired actions or reactions. They don't just happen; they are caused. Once the original cause of a habit is determined, it is within your power to accept or reject it. Most people allow their habits to control them. When those habits are hurtful, they negatively impact their attitudes.

The following steps will assist you in changing bad habits into good ones:

Step #1: List your bad habits.
Step #2: What was the original cause?

Step #3:   What are the supporting causes?

Step #4:   Determine a positive habit to replace the bad one.

Step #5:   Think about the good habit, its benefits and results.

Step #6:   Take action to develop this habit.

Step #7:   Daily act upon this habit for reinforcement.

Step #8:   Reward yourself by noting one of the benefits from your good habit.

CHOICE #8—CONTINUALLY CHOOSE TO HAVE A RIGHT ATTITUDE

Once you make the choice to possess a good attitude, the work has only just begun. After that comes a life of continually deciding to grow and maintaining the right outlook. Attitudes have a tendency to revert back to their original patterns if they are not carefully guarded and cultivated.

As you work to improve your attitude or to help the attitude of someone you lead, recognize that there are three stages of change where a person must deliberately choose the right attitude:

Early Stage: The first few days are always the most difficult. Old habits are hard to break. You must continually be on guard mentally to take the right action.

Middle Stage: The moment good habits begin to take root,

options open that bring on new challenges. During this stage, new habits will form that can be good or bad. The good news is that the more right choices and habits you develop, the more likely other good habits will be formed.

Later Stage: In the later stage, complacency is the enemy. We all know someone (perhaps us) who lost weight only to fall back into old eating habits and gain it back. Don't let down your guard until the change is complete. And even then, be vigilant and make sure you don't fall into old negative habits.

You are the only one who can determine what you will think and how you will act. And that means you can make your attitude what you want it to be. But even if you succeed and become a positive person, that won't shield you from negative experiences. How does a positive person deal with obstacles and remain upbeat? To find the answer to that question, read the next chapter.

5

———

CAN OBSTACLES ACTUALLY
ENHANCE AN ATTITUDE?

*The greatest battle you wage against failure occurs
on the inside, not the outside.*

Working artists David Bayles and Ted Orland tell a story about an art teacher who did an experiment with his grading system for two groups of students. It is a parable on the benefits of failure. Here is what happened:

The ceramics teacher announced on opening day that he was dividing the class into two groups. All those on the left side of the studio, he said, would be graded solely on the quantity of work they produced, all those on the right solely on its quality. His procedure was simple: on the final day of class he would bring in his bathroom scale and weigh the work of the "quantity" group: fifty pounds of pots rated an "A," forty pounds a "B," and so on. Those being graded on "quality," however, needed to produce only one pot—albeit a perfect one—to get an "A." Well, come grading time and a curious fact emerged:

the works of the highest quality were all produced by the group being graded for quantity. It seems that while the "quantity" group was busily churning out piles of work—and learning from their mistakes—the "quality" group had sat theorizing about perfection, and in the end had little more to show for their efforts than grandiose theories and a pile of dead clay.[1]

It doesn't matter whether your objectives are in the area of art, business, ministry, sports, or relationships. The only way you can get ahead is to fail early, fail often, and fail forward.

Take the Journey

I teach leadership to thousands of people each year at numerous conferences. And one of my greatest concerns is always that some people will go home from the event and nothing will change in their lives. They enjoy the "show" but fail to implement any of the ideas that were presented to them. I tell people continually: We overestimate the event and underestimate the process. Every dream that anyone has achieved came because of dedication to a process. (That's one of the reasons I write books and create audio programs—so that people can engage in the ongoing process of growth.)

People naturally tend toward inertia. That's why self-improvement is such a struggle. But that's also the reason that adversity lies at the heart of every success. The process of achievement comes through repeated failures and the constant struggle to climb to a higher level.

IN ORDER TO ACHIEVE YOUR DREAMS,
YOU MUST EMBRACE ADVERSITY AND MAKE FAILURE A
REGULAR PART OF YOUR LIFE. IF YOU'RE NOT FAILING,
YOU'RE PROBABLY NOT REALLY MOVING FORWARD.

When it comes to facing failure, most people will grudgingly concede that any person must make it through some adversity in order to succeed. They'll acknowledge that you have to experience the occasional setback to make progress. But I believe that success comes only if you take that thought one step further. In order to achieve your dreams, you must embrace adversity and make failure a regular part of your life. If you're not failing, you're probably not really moving forward.

THE BENEFITS OF ADVERSITY

Psychologist Dr. Joyce Brothers asserts, "The person interested in success has to learn to view failure as a healthy, inevitable part of the process of getting to the top." Adversity and the failure that often results from it should not only be expected in the process of succeeding; they need to be viewed as an absolutely critical part of it. In fact, the benefits of adversity are many. Take a look at some of the key reasons to embrace adversity and persevere through it:

1. Adversity Creates Resilience

Nothing in life breeds resilience like adversity and failure. A study in *Time* magazine in the mid-1980s described the incredible resilience of a group of people who had lost their jobs three times because of plant closings. Psychologists expected them to be discouraged, but they were surprisingly optimistic. Their adversity had actually created an advantage. Because they had already lost a job and found a new one at least twice, they were better able to handle adversity than people who had worked for only one company and found themselves unemployed.[2]

2. Adversity Develops Maturity

Adversity can make you better if you don't let it make you bitter. Why? Because it promotes wisdom and maturity. American novelist William Saroyan said, "Good people are good because they've come to wisdom through failure. We get very little wisdom from success, you know."

As the world continues to change at a faster and faster rate, maturity with flexibility becomes increasingly important. Those qualities come from weathering difficulties. Harvard business school professor John Kotter says, "I can imagine a group of executives 20 years ago discussing a candidate for a top job and saying, 'This guy had a big failure when he was 32.' Everyone else would say, 'Yep, yep, that's a bad sign.' I can imagine that same group considering a candidate today and saying, 'What worries me about this guy is that he's never failed.'"[3] The problems we face and overcome prepare us for future difficulties.

3. ADVERSITY PUSHES THE ENVELOPE OF ACCEPTED PERFORMANCE

Lloyd Ogilvie says that a friend of his, who was a circus performer in his youth, described his experience of learning to work on the trapeze as follows:

Once you know that the net below will catch you, you stop worrying about falling. You actually learn to fall successfully! What that means is, you can concentrate on catching the trapeze swinging toward you, and not on falling, because repeated falls in the past have convinced you that the net is strong and reliable when you do fall . . . The result of falling and being caught by the net is a mysterious confidence and daring on the trapeze. You fall less. Each fall makes you able to risk more.[4]

Until a person learns from personal experience that he

can live through adversity, he is reluctant to buck mindless tradition, push the envelope of organizational performance, or challenge himself to press his physical limits. Failure helps prompt people to rethink the status quo.

4. ADVERSITY PROVIDES GREATER OPPORTUNITIES

I believe that eliminating problems limits our potential. Just about every successful entrepreneur I've met has numerous stories of adversity and setbacks that opened doors to greater opportunity. For example, in 1978 Bernie Marcus, the son of a poor Russian cabinetmaker in Newark, New Jersey, was fired from Handy Dan, a do-it-yourself hardware retailer. That prompted Marcus to team with Arthur Blank to start their own business. In 1979, they opened their first store in Atlanta, Georgia. It was called Home Depot. Today, Home Depot has more than 760 stores employing more than 157,000 people; they have expanded the business to include overseas operations; and each year they do more than $30 billion in sales.

I'm sure Bernie Marcus wasn't very happy about getting fired from his job back at Handy Dan. But if he hadn't been, who knows whether he would have achieved the success he has today.

5. ADVERSITY PROMPTS INNOVATION

Early in the twentieth century, a boy whose family had

emigrated from Sweden to Illinois sent twenty-five cents to a publisher for a book on photography. What he received instead was a book on ventriloquism. What did he do? He adapted and learned ventriloquism. He was Edgar Bergen, and for over forty years he entertained audiences with the help of a wooden dummy named Charlie McCarthy.

The ability to innovate is at the heart of creativity—a vital component in success. University of Houston professor Jack Matson recognized that fact and developed a course that his students call "Failure 101." In it, Matson has students build mock-ups of products that no one would ever buy. His goal is to get students to equate failure with innovation instead of defeat. That way they will free themselves to try new things. "They learn to reload and get ready to shoot again," says Matson. If you want to succeed, you have to learn to make adjustments to the way you do things and try again. Adversity helps to develop that ability.

6. ADVERSITY BRINGS UNEXPECTED BENEFITS

The average person makes a mistake, and automatically thinks that it's a failure. But some of the greatest stories of success can be found in the unexpected benefits of mistakes. For example, most people are familiar with the story of Edison and the phonograph: He discovered it while trying to invent something entirely different. But did you also know that Kellogg's Corn Flakes resulted when boiled wheat was left in a baking pan overnight? Or that Ivory soap floats because a batch was left in the mixer too long and had a large volume of air whipped into it? Or that Scott Towels were launched when a toilet paper machine put too many layers of tissue together?

"IN SCIENCE, MISTAKES ALWAYS PRECEDE THE TRUTH."
—HORACE WALPOLE

Horace Walpole said that "in science, mistakes always precede the truth." That's what happened to German-Swiss chemist Christian Friedrich Schönbein. One day he was working in the kitchen—which his wife had strictly forbidden—and was experimenting with sulfuric and nitric acid. When he accidentally spilled some of the mixture on the kitchen table, he thought he was in trouble. (He knew he would experience "adversity" when his wife found out!) He hurriedly snatched up a cotton apron, wiped up the mess, and hung the apron by the fire to dry.

Suddenly there was a violent explosion. Evidently the cellulose in the cotton underwent a process called "nitration." Unwittingly, Schönbein had invented nitrocellulose—what came to be called smokeless gunpowder or gun-cotton. He went on to market his invention, which made him a lot of money.

7. ADVERSITY MOTIVATES

Years ago when Bear Bryant was coaching the University of Alabama's football team, the Crimson Tide was ahead by only six points in a game with less than two minutes remaining in the fourth quarter. Bryant sent his quarterback into the game with instructions to play it safe and run out the clock.

In the huddle, the quarterback said, "Coach says to play it safe, but that's what they're expecting. Let's give them a surprise." And with that, he called a pass play.

When the quarterback dropped back and threw the pass, the defending cornerback, who was a champion sprinter, intercepted the ball and headed for the end zone expecting to score a touchdown. The quarterback, who was not known as a good runner, took off after the cornerback and ran him down from behind, tackling him on the five-yard line. It saved the game.

After the clock ran out, the opposing coach approached Bear Bryant and said, "What's this business about your quarterback not being a runner? He ran down my speedster from behind!"

Bryant responded, "Your man was running for six points. My man was running for his life."

Nothing can motivate a person like adversity. Olympic diver Pat McCormick said, "I think failure is one of the great motivators. After my narrow loss in the 1948 trials, I knew how really good I could be. It was the defeat that focused all my concentration on my training and goals." McCormick went on to win two gold medals in the Olympics in London that year and another two in Helsinki four years later.

If you can step back from the negative circumstances you face in life, you will be able to discover that there are positive benefits to your negative experiences. That is almost always true; you simply have to be willing to look for them—and not take the adversity you are experiencing too personally.

So if you lose your job, think about the resilience you're developing. If you try something daring and survive, think about what you learned about yourself—and how it will help you take on new challenges. If a restaurant gets your order wrong, figure out if it's an opportunity to learn a new skill. And if you experience a train wreck in your career, think of the maturity it's developing in you. Besides, Bill Vaughan says, "In the game of life it's a good idea to have a few early losses, which relieves you of the pressure of trying to maintain an undefeated season." Always measure an obstacle next to the size of the dream you're pursuing. It's all in how you look at it. Try, and you can find the good in every bad experience.

WHAT COULD BE WORSE?

One of the most incredible stories of adversity overcome and success gained is that of Joseph of the ancient Hebrews. You may be familiar with the story. He was born the eleventh of twelve sons in a wealthy Middle Eastern family whose trade was raising livestock. As a teenager, Joseph alienated his brothers: First, he was his father's favorite, even though he was nearly the youngest. Second, he used to tell his father any time his brothers weren't doing their work properly with the sheep. And third, he made the mistake of telling his older brothers that one day he would be in charge of them. At first a group of his brothers wanted to kill him, but the eldest, Reuben, prevented them from doing that. So when Reuben wasn't around, the others sold him into slavery.

Joseph ended up in Egypt working in the house of the captain of the guard, a man named Potiphar. Because of his leadership and administrative skill, Joseph quickly rose in the ranks, and before long, he was running the entire household. He was making the best of a bad situation. But then things got worse. The wife of his master tried to persuade him to sleep with her. When he refused, she accused him of making advances toward her, and got Potiphar to throw Joseph in prison.

FROM SLAVERY TO PRISON

At that point Joseph was in about as difficult a position as he could be. He was separated from his family. He was living away from home in a foreign land. He was a slave. And he was in prison. But again, he made the best of a tough situation. Before long, the warden of the prison put Joseph in charge of all the prisoners and all the prison's daily activities.

While in prison, Joseph got the chance to meet a fellow prisoner who had been an official from Pharaoh's court, the chief cupbearer. And Joseph was able to do him a favor by interpreting a dream the man had. When he saw that the official was grateful, Joseph made a request of him in return.

"When all goes well with you," Joseph asked, "remember me and show me kindness; mention me to Pharaoh and get me out of this prison. For I was forcibly carried off from the land of the Hebrews, and even here I have done nothing to deserve being put in a dungeon."[5]

Joseph had great hope a few days later when the official was returned to court and the good graces of the monarch. He expected any minute to receive word that Pharaoh was setting him free. But he waited. And waited. Two years passed before the cupbearer remembered Joseph, and he did so only because Pharaoh wanted someone to interpret one of his dreams.

FINALLY . . . THE PAYOFF

In the end, Joseph was able to interpret Pharaoh's dreams. And because the Hebrew showed such great wisdom, the Egyptian ruler put Joseph in charge of the entire kingdom. As the result of Joseph's leadership, planning, and system of food storage, when famine struck the Middle East seven years later, many thousands of people who otherwise would have died were able to survive—including Joseph's own family. When his brothers traveled to Egypt for relief from the famine—twenty years after selling him into slavery—they discovered that their brother Joseph was not only alive, but second in command of the most powerful kingdom in the world.

Few people would welcome the adversity of thirteen years in bondage as a slave and prisoner. But as far as we know, Joseph never gave up hope and never lost his perspective. Nor did he hold a grudge against his brothers. After their father died, he told them, "You intended to harm me, but God intended it for good to accomplish what is now being done, the saving of many lives."

Joseph found the positive benefits in his negative experiences. And if he can do it, so can we. To help you do that, you need to take the next step when it comes to attitude. You have to be able to deal positively with failure.

PART III

THE FUTURE WITH THE RIGHT ATTITUDE

6

WHAT IS FAILURE?

Every successful person is someone who failed,
yet never regarded himself as a failure.

In an interview years ago David Brinkley asked advice columnist Ann Landers what question she most frequently received from readers. Her answer: "What's wrong with me?"

Landers's response reveals a lot about human nature. Many people wrestle with feelings of failure, the most damaging being doubtful thoughts about themselves. At the heart of those doubts and feelings is one central question: Am I a failure? And that's a problem because I believe it's nearly impossible for any person to believe he is a failure and succeed at the same time. Instead, you have to meet failure with the right attitude and determine to fail forward.

It seems that advice columnists (such as the late Ann Landers) and humor writers recognize that keeping a good attitude about yourself is important to overcoming adversity and mistakes. The late Erma Bombeck, who wrote a widely syndicated weekly humor column until a few weeks before her death in 1996, had a firm grasp on what it meant to persevere and fail forward without taking failure too personally.

FROM NEWSPAPER COPY GIRL TO *TIME* MAGAZINE COVER GIRL

Erma Bombeck traveled a road that was filled with adversity, starting with her career. She was drawn to journalism early in life. Her first job was as a copy girl at the *Dayton Journal-Herald* when she was a teenager. But when she went off to college at Ohio University, a guidance counselor advised her, "Forget about writing." She refused. Later she transferred to the University of Dayton and in 1949 graduated with a degree in English. Soon afterward she began working as a writer—for the obituary column and the women's page.

That year adversity carried over into her personal life. When she got married, one of her deepest desires was to become a mother. But much to her dismay, her doctors told her she was incapable of having children. Did she give up and consider herself a failure? No, she and her husband explored the possibility of adoption, and then they adopted a daughter.

Two years later, a surprised Erma became pregnant. But even that brought her more difficulties. In four years she experienced four pregnancies, but only two of the babies survived.

In 1964 Erma was able to convince the editor of a small neighborhood newspaper, the *Kettering-Oakwood Times*, to let her write a weekly humor column. Despite the pitiful $3 per article she was paid, she kept writing. And that opened a door for her. The next year she was offered the opportunity to write a three-times-a-week column for her old employer, the *Dayton Journal-Herald*. By 1967 her column was syndicated and carried by more than nine hundred newspapers.

For slightly more than thirty years Erma wrote her humor column. During that time she published fifteen books, was recognized as one of the twenty-five most influential women in America, appeared frequently on the television show *Good Morning America*, was featured on the cover of *Time* magazine, received innumerable honors (such as the American Cancer Society's Medal of Honor), and was awarded fifteen honorary degrees.

More Than Her Share of Problems

But during that span of time, Erma Bombeck also experienced incredible troubles and trials, including breast cancer, a mastectomy, and kidney failure. And she wasn't shy about sharing her perspective on her life experiences:

I speak at college commencements, and I tell everyone I'm up there and they're down there, not because of my successes, but my failures. Then I proceed to spin all of them off—a comedy record album that sold two copies in Beirut . . . a sitcom that lasted about as long as a donut in our house . . . a Broadway play that never saw Broadway . . . book signings where I attracted two people: one who wanted directions to the restroom and the other who wanted to buy the desk.

What you have to tell yourself is, "I'm not a failure. I failed at doing something." There's a big difference . . . Personally and career-wise, it's been a corduroy road. I've buried babies, lost parents, had cancer, and worried over kids. The trick is to put it all in perspective . . . and that's what I do for a living.[1]

That winning attitude kept Erma Bombeck down to earth. (She liked to refer to herself as "a former homeroom mother and obituary writer.") It also kept her going—and writing—through the disappointments, the pain, the surgeries, and the daily kidney dialysis until her death at age sixty-nine.

EVERY GENIUS COULD HAVE BEEN A "FAILURE"

Every successful person is someone who failed, yet never regarded himself as a failure. For example, Wolfgang Mozart, one of the geniuses of musical composition, was told by Emperor Ferdinand that his opera *The Marriage of Figaro* was "far too noisy" and contained "far too many notes." Artist Vincent van Gogh, whose paintings now set records for the sums they bring at auction, sold only one painting in his lifetime. Thomas Edison, the most prolific inventor in history, was considered unteachable as a youngster. And Albert Einstein, the greatest thinker of our time, was told by a Munich schoolmaster that he would "never amount to much."

I think it's safe to say that all great achievers are given multiple reasons to believe they are failures. But in spite of that, they remain positive and they persevere. In the face of adversity, rejection, and failings, they continue believing in themselves and refuse to consider themselves failures. They chose to develop the right attitude about failure.

FAILING FORWARD IS NOT FALSE SELF-ESTEEM

I place high value on praising people, especially children. In fact, I believe that people live up to your level of expectation. But I also believe that you have to base your praise on truth. You don't make up nice things to say about others. Here's the approach I use to encourage and lead others:

> Value people.
> Praise effort.
> Reward performance.

I use that method with everyone. I even use a form of it with myself. When I'm working, I don't give myself a reward until after the job is finished. When I approach a task or project, I give it my very best, and no matter what the results are, I have a clear conscience. I have no problem sleeping at night. And no matter where I fail or how many mistakes I make, I don't let it devalue my worth as a person. As the saying goes, "God uses people who fail—'cause there aren't any other kind around."

It is possible to cultivate a positive attitude about yourself, no matter what circumstances you find yourself in or what kind of history you have.

SEVEN ABILITIES NEEDED TO FAIL FORWARD

Here are seven abilities of achievers that enable them to fail, not take it personally, and keep moving forward:

1. REJECT REJECTION

Author James Allen states, "A man is literally what he thinks, his character being the complete sum of all his thought." That's why it's important to make sure your thinking is on the right track.

People who don't give up keep trying because they don't base their self-worth on their performance. Instead, they have an internally based self-image. Rather than say, "I am a failure," they say, "I missed that one," or "I made a mistake."

Psychologist Martin E. Seligman believes we have two choices when we fail: We can internalize or externalize our failure. "People who blame themselves when they fail . . . think they are worthless, talentless, unlovable," says Seligman. "People who blame external events do not lose self-esteem when bad events strike."[2] To keep the right perspective, take responsibility for your actions, but don't take failure personally.

2. SEE FAILURE AS TEMPORARY

People who personalize failure see a problem as a hole they're permanently stuck in. But achievers see any predicament as temporary. For example, take the case of United States President Harry S. Truman. In 1922 he was thirty-eight years old, in debt, and out of work. In 1945 he was the most powerful leader of the free world, occupying the highest office in the land. If he had seen failure as permanent, he would have remained stuck and never would have kept trying and believing in his potential.

3. SEE FAILURES AS ISOLATED INCIDENTS

Author Leo Buscaglia once talked about his admiration for cooking expert Julia Child: "I just love her attitude. She says, 'Tonight we're going to make a soufflé!' And she beats this and whisks that, and she drops things on the floor . . . and does all these wonderful human things. Then she takes the soufflé and throws it in the oven and talks to you for a while. Finally, she says, 'Now it's ready!' But when she opens the oven, the soufflé just falls flat as a pancake. But does she panic or burst into tears? No! She smiles and says, 'Well, you can't win them all. Bon appetit!'"

When achievers fail, they see it as a momentary event, not a lifelong epidemic. It's not personal. If you want to succeed, don't let any single incident color your view of yourself.

4. KEEP EXPECTATIONS REALISTIC

The greater the feat you desire to achieve, the greater the mental preparation required for overcoming obstacles and persevering over the long haul. If you want to take a stroll in your neighborhood, you can reasonably expect to have few, if any, problems. But that's not the case if you intend to climb Mount Everest.

It takes time, effort, and the ability to overcome setbacks. You have to approach each day with reasonable expectations and not get your feelings hurt when everything doesn't turn out perfectly.

Something that happened on baseball's opening day in 1954 illustrates the point well. The Milwaukee Braves and the Cincinnati Reds played each other, and a rookie for each team made his major-league debut during that game. The rookie who played for the Reds hit four doubles and helped his team win with a score of 9-8. The rookie for the Braves went 0 for 5. The Reds player was Jim Greengrass, a name you probably haven't heard. The other guy, who didn't get a hit, might be more familiar to you. His name was Hank Aaron, the player who became the best home-run hitter in the history of baseball.

If Aaron's expectations for that first game had been unrealistic, who knows? He might have given up baseball. Surely he wasn't happy about his performance that day, but he didn't think of himself as a failure. He had worked too hard for too long. He wasn't about to give up easily.

5. FOCUS ON STRENGTHS

Another way achievers keep themselves from personalizing failure is by focusing on their strengths. Bob Butera, former president of the New Jersey Devils hockey team, was asked what makes a winner. He answered, "What distinguishes winners from losers is that winners concentrate at all times on what they can do, not on what they can't do. If a guy is a great shooter but not a great skater, we tell him to think only about the shot, the shot, the shot—never about some other guy outskating him. The idea is to remember your successes."

If a weakness is a matter of character, it needs much attention. Focus on it until you shore it up. Otherwise, the best bet for failing forward is developing and maximizing your strengths.

6. VARY APPROACHES TO ACHIEVEMENT

In *The Psychology of Achievement*, Brian Tracy writes about four millionaires who made their fortunes by age thirty-five. They were involved in an average of seventeen businesses before finding the one that took them to the top. They kept trying and changing until they found something that worked for them.

Achievers are willing to vary their approaches to problems. That's important in every walk of life, not just business. For example, if you're a fan of track-and-field events, you have undoubtedly enjoyed watching athletes compete in the high jump. I'm always amazed by the heights achieved by the men and women in that event. What's really interesting is that in the 1960s, the sport went through a major change in technique that allowed athletes to break the old records and push them up to new levels.

The person responsible for that change was Dick Fosbury. Where previous athletes used the straddle method to high jump, in which they went over the bar while facing it, with one arm and one leg leading, Fosbury developed a technique where he went over headfirst with his back to the bar. It was dubbed the Fosbury Flop.

Developing a new high-jump technique was one thing. Getting it accepted by others was another matter. Fosbury remarked, "I was told over and over again that I would never be successful, that I was not going to be competitive and the technique was simply not going to work. All I could do was shrug and say, 'We'll just have to see.'"

And people did see. Fosbury won the gold medal in the Mexico City Olympics in 1968, shattering the previous Olympic record and setting a new world record in the process. Since then, nearly all world-class high jumpers have used his technique. To achieve his goals, Fosbury varied his approach to high jumping, and he kept a positive attitude by not allow-ing others' comments to make him feel like a failure.

7. BOUNCE BACK

All achievers have in common the ability to bounce back after an error, mistake, or failure. Psychologist Simone

Caruthers says, "Life is a series of outcomes. Sometimes the outcome is what you want. Great. Figure out what you did right. Sometimes the outcome is what you don't want. Great. Figure out what you did so you don't do it again."[3] The key to bouncing back is found in your attitude toward the outcome.

Achievers are able to keep moving forward no matter what happens. And that's made possible because they remember that failure does not make *them* failures. No one should take mistakes personally. That's the best way to pick yourself up after failure and continue with a positive attitude. Once you do that, you're ready for success, which happens to be the subject of the next chapter.

7

WHAT IS SUCCESS?

*Attitude determines how far you can go
on the success journey.*

D o you want to be successful? The problem for most
people who want to be successful is *not* that they can't
achieve success. The main obstacle for them is that they misunderstand success. They don't have the right *attitude* about
it. Maltbie D. Babcock said, "One of the most common mistakes and one of the costliest is thinking that success is due to
some genius, some magic, something or other which we do
not possess."

What is success? What does it look like? Most people have
a vague picture of what it means to be a successful person that
looks something like this:

The wealth of Bill Gates,
the physique of Arnold Schwarzenegger,
(or Tyra Banks),
the intelligence of Albert Einstein,

the athletic ability of Michael Jordan,
the business prowess of Donald Trump,
the social grace and poise of Jackie Kennedy,
the imagination of Walt Disney, and
the heart of Mother Teresa.

That sounds absurd, but it's closer to the truth than we would like to admit. Many of us picture success as looking like someone other than who we are. That's the wrong way to think about it. If you tried to become just like even one of these other people, you wouldn't be successful. You would be a bad imitation of them, and you would eliminate the possibility of becoming the person you were meant to be.

THE WRONG ATTITUDE ABOUT SUCCESS

Even if you avoid the trap of thinking that success means being like some other person, you might still have a wrong attitude toward success. Many people wrongly equate it with achievement of some sort, with arriving at a destination or attaining a goal. Here are several of the most common misconceptions about success:

WEALTH

Probably the most common misunderstanding about success is that it's the same as having money. A lot of people believe that if they accumulate wealth, they will be successful. But wealth doesn't eliminate current problems, and it introduces many new ones. If you don't believe that, look at the lives of lottery winners. Wealth does not bring contentment or success.

A SPECIAL FEELING

Another common misconception is that people have achieved success when they feel successful or happy. But trying to *feel* successful is probably even more difficult than trying to become wealthy. The continual search for happiness is a primary reason that so many people are miserable. If you make happiness your goal, you are almost certainly destined to fail. You will be on a continual roller coaster, changing from successful to unsuccessful with every mood change. Life is uncertain, and emotions aren't stable. Happiness simply cannot be relied upon as a measure of success.

SPECIFIC AND WORTHWHILE POSSESSIONS

Think back to when you were a kid. Chances are that there was a time when you wanted something badly, and you believed that if you possessed that thing, it would make a significant difference in your life. When I was nine years old, it was a burgundy-and-silver Schwinn bicycle, which I received for Christmas. But I soon discovered that it didn't bring me the success or long-term contentment that I hoped for and expected.

That process has repeated itself in my life. I found that success didn't come when I became a starter on my high school basketball team, when I became the student body president in college, or when I bought my first house. It has never come as the result of possessing something I wanted. Possessions are at best a temporary fix. Success cannot be attained or measured that way.

POWER

Charles McElroy once joked, "Power is usually recognized as an excellent short-term antidepressant." That statement contains a lot of truth because power often gives the appearance of success, but even then, it's only temporary.

You've probably heard before the quote from English historian Lord Acton: "Power tends to corrupt and absolute power corrupts absolutely." Abraham Lincoln echoed that belief when he said, "Nearly all men can stand adversity, but if you want to test a man's character, give him power." Power really is a test of character. In the hands of a person of integrity, it is of tremendous benefit; in the hands of a tyrant, it causes terrible destruction. By itself, power is neither positive nor negative. And it is not the source of security or success. Besides, all dictators—even benevolent ones—eventually lose power.

Achievement

Many people have what I call "destination disease." They believe that if they can arrive somewhere—attain a position, accomplish a goal, or have a relationship with the right person—they will be successful. At one time I had a similar view of success. I defined it as the progressive realization of a predetermined worthwhile goal. But over time I realized that the definition fell short of the mark. Success isn't a list of goals to be checked off one after another. It's not reaching a destination. Success is a journey.

The Right Attitude About Success

If success is a journey, how do you get started? What does it take to be successful? Two things are required: the right attitude toward success and the right principles for getting there. Once you redefine success as a journey, you can maintain the right attitude toward it. Then you're ready to start the process. The results may be as unique as each individual, but the process is the same for everyone. Here is my definition of success:

> *Success is . . .*
> *Knowing your purpose in life,*
> *Growing to reach your maximum potential, and*
> *Sowing seeds that benefit others.*

When you think of success in this way, you can see why it must be seen as a journey rather than a destination. No matter how long you live or what you decide to do in life, as long as you have the right attitude about it, you will never exhaust your capacity to grow toward your potential or run out of opportunities to help others. When you see success as a journey, you'll never have the problem of trying to "arrive" at an elusive final destination. And you'll never find yourself in a position where you have accomplished some final goal, only to discover that you're still unfulfilled and searching for something else to do.

To get a better handle on these aspects of success, let's take a look at each one of them:

KNOWING YOUR PURPOSE

Nothing can take the place of knowing your purpose. Millionaire industrialist Henry J. Kaiser, the founder of Kaiser Aluminum as well as the Kaiser-Permanente health care system, said, "The evidence is overwhelming that you cannot begin to achieve your best unless you set some aim in life." Or put another way, if you don't try actively to discover your purpose, you're likely to spend your life doing the wrong things.

I believe that God created every person for a purpose. According to psychologist Viktor Frankl, "Everyone has his own specific vocation or mission in life. Everyone must carry out a concrete assignment that demands fulfillment. Therein he cannot be replaced, nor can his life be repeated. Thus everyone's task is as unique as his specific opportunity to implement it." Each of us has a purpose for which we were created. Our responsibility—and our greatest joy—is to identify it.

Here are some questions to ask yourself to help you identify your purpose:

For what am I searching? All of us have a strong desire buried in our hearts, something that speaks to our deepest thoughts and feelings, something that sets our souls on fire. You only need to find it.

Why was I created? Each of us is different. Think about your unique mix of abilities, the resources available to you, your personal history, and the opportunities around you. If you objectively identify these factors and discover the desire of your heart, you will have done a lot toward discovering your purpose in life.

Do I believe in my potential? If you don't believe that you have potential, you will never try to reach it. You should take the advice of President Theodore Roosevelt, who said, "Do what you can, with what you have, where you are." If you do that with your eyes fixed on your life purpose, what else can be expected of you?

When do I start? The answer to that question is NOW.

GROWING TO YOUR POTENTIAL

Novelist H. G. Wells held that wealth, notoriety, place, and power are no measures of success whatsoever. The only true measure of success is the ratio between what we might have been and what we have become. In other words, success comes as the result of growing to our potential.

We have nearly limitless potential, yet too few ever try to reach it. Why? The answer lies in this: We can do *anything*, but we can't do *everything*. Many people let everyone around them decide their agenda in life. As a result, they never really dedicate themselves to *their* purpose in life. They become a jack-of-all-trades, master of none—rather than a jack-of-few-trades, focused on one.

If that describes you more than you'd like, you're probably ready to take steps to make a change. Here are four principles to put you on the road to growing toward your potential:

1. CONCENTRATE ON ONE MAIN GOAL.

Nobody ever reached her potential by scattering herself in twenty directions. Reaching your potential requires focus.

2. CONCENTRATE ON CONTINUAL IMPROVEMENT.

David D. Glass, chairman of the executive committee of the Wal-Mart board of directors, was once asked whom he admired most. His answer was Wal-Mart founder Sam Walton. He remarked, "There's never been a day in his life, since I've known him, that he didn't improve in some way." Commitment to continual improvement is the key to reaching your potential and to being successful.

3. FORGET THE PAST.

My friend Jack Hayford, pastor of Church on the Way in Van Nuys, California, commented, "The past is a dead issue, and we can't gain any momentum moving toward tomorrow if we are dragging the past behind us."

If you need inspiration, think of other people who overcame seemingly insurmountable obstacles, such as Booker T. Washington, Helen Keller, and Franklin Delano Roosevelt. Each of them overcame incredible odds to achieve great things. And remember, no matter what you've faced in the past, you have the *potential* to overcome it.

4. FOCUS ON THE FUTURE.

Baseball Hall of Famer Yogi Berra declared, "The future isn't what it used to be." Although that may be true, it's still the only place we have to go. Your potential lies ahead of you—whether you're eight, eighteen, forty-eight, or eighty. You still have room to improve yourself. You can become better tomorrow than you are today. As the

Spanish proverb says, "He who does not look ahead remains behind."

Sowing Seeds That Benefit Others

When you know your purpose in life and are growing to reach your maximum potential, you're well on your way to being a success. But there is one more essential part of the success journey: helping others. Without that aspect, the journey can be a lonely and shallow experience.

It's been said that we make a living by what we get, but we make a life by what we give. Physician, theologian, and philosopher Albert Schweitzer stated it even more strongly: "The purpose of human life is to serve, and to show compassion and the will to help others." For him, the success journey led to Africa where he served people for many years.

For you, sowing seeds that benefit others probably won't mean traveling to another country to serve the poor—unless that is the purpose you were born to fulfill. (And if it is, you won't be satisfied until that's what you're doing.) However, if you're like most people, helping others is something you can do right here at home, whether it's spending more time with your family, developing an employee who shows potential, helping people in the community, or putting your desires on hold for the sake of your team at work. The key is to find your purpose and help others while you're pursuing it. Entertainer Danny Thomas insisted that "all of us are born for a reason, but all of us don't discover why. Success in life has nothing to do with what you gain in life or accomplish for yourself. It's what you do for others."

WE MAKE A LIVING BY WHAT WE GET;
BUT WE MAKE A LIFE BY WHAT WE GIVE.

Having the right view of success can help you keep a positive attitude about yourself and life, no matter what kind of circumstances you find yourself in. And if you can help the people you lead to adopt that same view of success, you can help them to always have hope and to become successful. Why? Because all people—regardless of talent level, education, or upbringing—are capable of knowing their purpose, growing to their maximum potential, and sowing seeds that benefit others. And helping people is what leadership is really all about.

But there's one more truth you need to know if you want to be a successful leader in the area of attitude. And you'll find that in the last chapter.

8

How Can a Leader
Keep Climbing?

Leaders have to give up to go up.

M any people today want to climb up the corporate ladder because they believe that freedom and power are the prizes waiting at the top. What they don't realize is that the true nature of leadership is really sacrifice.

Most people will acknowledge that sacrifices are necessary fairly early in a leadership career. People give up many things in order to gain potential opportunities. For example, Tom Murphy began working for General Motors in 1937. But he almost refused the first position he was offered with the company because the one-hundred-dollar-a-month salary barely covered his expenses. Despite his misgivings, he took the job anyway, thinking the opportunity was worth the sacrifice. He was right. Murphy eventually became General Motors' chairman of the board.

Sacrifice is a constant in leadership. It is an ongoing process, not a one-time payment. It's an attitude that any successful leader must maintain. When I look back at my career, I recognize that there has always been a cost involved in moving forward. That's been true for me in the area of finances with every career change I've made since I was twenty-two years old. Any time you know that the step is right, don't hesitate to make a sacrifice.

You've Got to Give Up to Go Up

Leaders who want to rise have to do more than take an occasional cut in pay. They have to give up their rights. As my friend Gerald Brooks says, "When you become a leader, you lose the right to think about yourself." For every person, the nature of the sacrifice may be different. Leaders give up to go up. That's true of every leader regardless of profession. Talk to any leader, and you will find that he has made repeated sacrifices. Usually, the higher that leader has climbed, the greater the sacrifices he has made.

The Higher You Go, the More You Give Up

Who is the most powerful leader in the world? I'd say it's the president of the United States. More than any other single person, his actions and words make an impact on people, not just in our country, but around the globe. Think about what he must give up to reach the office of president and then to hold that office. His time is no longer his own. He is scrutinized constantly. His family is under tremendous pressure. And as a matter of course, he must make decisions that can cost thousands of people their lives. Even after he leaves office, he will spend the rest of his life in the company of Secret Service agents who protect him from bodily harm.

The greater the leader, the more he must give up. Think about someone like Martin Luther King, Jr. His wife, Coretta Scott King, remarked in *My Life with Martin Luther King, Jr.*, "Day and night our phone would ring, and someone would pour out a string of obscene epithets . . . Frequently the calls ended with a threat to kill us if we didn't get out of town. But in spite of all the danger, the chaos of our private lives, I felt inspired, almost elated."

While pursuing his course of leadership during the civil rights movement, King was arrested and jailed on many occasions. He was stoned, stabbed, and physically attacked. His house was bombed. Yet his vision—and his influence—continued to increase. Ultimately, he sacrificed everything he had. But what he gave up he parted with willingly. In his last speech, delivered the night before his assassination in Memphis, he said,

I don't know what will happen to me now. We've got some difficult days ahead. But it doesn't matter to me now. Because

I've been to the mountaintop. I won't mind. Like anybody else, I would like to live a long life. Longevity has its place. But I'm not concerned about that now. I just want to do God's will. And He's allowed me to go up to the mountain. And I've looked over and I've seen the Promised Land. I may not get there with you, but I want you to know tonight that we, as a people, will get to the Promised Land. So I'm happy tonight . . . I'm not fearing any man. "Mine eyes have seen the glory of the coming of the Lord."[1]

The next day he paid the ultimate price of sacrifice. King's impact was profound. He influenced millions of people to peacefully stand up against a system and society that fought to exclude them.

THE HIGHER THE LEVEL OF LEADERSHIP YOU WANT
TO REACH, THE GREATER THE SACRIFICES
YOU WILL HAVE TO MAKE.

What successful people find to be true becomes even clearer to them when they become leaders. There is no success without an attitude of sacrifice. The higher the level of leadership you want to reach, the greater the sacrifices you will have to make. To go up, you have to give up. That is the true nature of leadership. That is the power of the right attitude.

NOTES

Chapter 1
1. John C. Maxwell, *The Winning Attitude* (Nashville: Thomas Nelson, 1993), 24.
2. Denis Waitley, *The Winner's Edge* (New York: Berkley Publishing Group, 1994).
3. Pat Riley, *The Winner Within* (New York: Berkley Publishing Group, 1994), 41, 52.

Chapter 2
1. Galatians 6:7.
2. J. Sidlow Baxter, *Awake, My Heart* (Grand Rapids: Kregal Publications, 1996).
3. See Luke 15:29–30.

Chapter 4
1. Proverbs 23:7.
2. Philippians 4:8.

Chapter 5
1. David Bayles and Ted Orland, *Art and Fear: Observations on the Perils (And Rewards) of Artmaking* (Santa Barbara: Capra Press, 1993), 29.

2. Arthur Freeman and Rose Dewolf, *Woulda, Coulda, Shoulda: Overcoming Regrets, Mistakes, and Missed Opportunities* (New York: HarperCollins, 1992).

3. Patricia Sellers, "Now Bounce Back!" *Fortune*, May 1, 1995, 49.

4. Lloyd Ogilvie, *Falling into Greatness* (Nashville: Thomas Nelson, 1984).

5. Genesis 40:14–15 NIV.

Chapter 6

1. Andy Andrews, ed., "Erma Bombeck" in *Storms of Perfection 2* (Nashville: Lightning Crown Publishers, 1994), 51.

2. Brodin, "The Key to Bouncing Back," *Discipleship Journal*, issue 109, 1999, 67.

3. "Where Failures Get Fixed," *Fortune*, May 1, 1995, 64.

Chapter 7

1. David Wallechinsky, *The Twentieth Century* (Boston: Little, Brown, 1995), 155.

LEADERSHIP

101

WHAT EVERY LEADER NEEDS TO KNOW

JOHN C. MAXWELL

NELSON BUSINESS
A Division of Thomas Nelson Publishers
Since 1798

www.thomasnelson.com

Published in Nashville, Tennessee, by Thomas Nelson, Inc.

Portions of this book were previously published in *Becoming a Person of
Influence, The 21 Irrefutable Laws of Leadership, The 21 Indispensable
Qualities of a Leader,* and *Developing the Leader Within You.*

Library of Congress Cataloging-in-Publication

Maxwell, John C., 1947–
Leadership 101 / John C. Maxwell.
p. cm.
ISBN 0-7852-6419-1 (hc)
1. Leadership. I. Title: Leadership one hundred one. II. Title.
HM1261 .M3897 2002
303.3'4—dc21
2002009572

CONTENTS

Part 1

The Development
of a Leader

I

WHY SHOULD I GROW AS A LEADER?

*The higher the leadership,
the greater the effectiveness.*

I often open my leadership conferences by explaining what I call the Law of the Lid because it helps people understand the value of leadership. If you can get a handle on this principle, you will see the incredible impact of leadership on every aspect of life. So here it is: Leadership ability is the lid that determines a person's level of effectiveness. The lower an individual's ability to lead, the lower the lid on his potential. The higher the leadership, the greater the effectiveness. To give you an example, if your leadership rates an 8, then your effectiveness can never be greater than a 7. If your leadership is only a 4, then your effectiveness will be no higher than a 3. Your leadership ability—for better or for worse—always determines your effectiveness and the potential impact of your organization.

Let me tell you a story that illustrates the Law of the Lid.

In 1930, two young brothers named Dick and Maurice moved from New Hampshire to California in search of the American Dream. They had just gotten out of high school, and they saw few opportunities back home. So they headed straight for Hollywood where they eventually found jobs on a movie studio set.

After a while, their entrepreneurial spirit and interest in the entertainment industry prompted them to open a theater in Glendale, a town about five miles northeast of Hollywood. But despite all their efforts, the brothers just couldn't make the business profitable, so they looked for a better business opportunity.

A NEW OPPORTUNITY

In 1937, the brothers opened a small drive-in restaurant in Pasadena, located just east of Glendale. As people in southern California became more dependent on their cars in the thirties, drive-in restaurants sprang up everywhere. Customers would drive into a parking lot around a small restaurant, place their orders with carhops, and receive their food on trays right in their cars. The food was served on china plates complete with glassware and metal utensils.

Dick and Maurice's tiny drive-in restaurant was a great success, and in 1940, they moved the operation to San

Bernardino, a working-class boomtown fifty miles east of Los Angeles. They built a larger facility and expanded their menu from hot dogs, fries, and shakes to include barbecued beef and pork sandwiches, hamburgers, and other items. Their business exploded. Annual sales reached $200,000, and the brothers found themselves splitting $50,000 in profits every year—a sum that put them in the town's financial elite.

By 1948, their intuition told them that times were changing, so they made modifications to their restaurant business. They eliminated the carhops and started serving only walk-up customers. They reduced their menu and focused on selling hamburgers. They eliminated plates, glassware, and metal utensils, switching to paper products instead. They reduced their costs and the prices they charged customers. They also created what they called the Speedy Service System. Their kitchen became like an assembly line, where each person focused on service with speed. Their goal was to fill each customer's order in thirty seconds or less. And they succeeded. By the mid-1950s, annual revenue hit $350,000, and by then, Dick and Maurice split net profits of about $100,000 each year.

Who were these brothers? On the front of their small restaurant hung a neon sign that said simply MCDONALD'S HAMBURGERS. Dick and Maurice McDonald had hit the great American jackpot, and the rest, as they say, is history, right? Wrong. The McDonalds never went any farther because their weak leadership put a lid on their ability to succeed.

THE STORY BEHIND THE STORY

It's true that the McDonald brothers were financially secure. Theirs was one of the most profitable restaurant enterprises in the country, and their genius was in customer service and kitchen organization, which led to a new system of food and beverage service. In fact, their talent was so widely known in food service circles that people from all over the country wanted to learn more about their methods. At one point, they received as many as three hundred calls and letters every month. That led them to the idea of marketing the McDonald's concept.

The idea of franchising restaurants had been around for several decades. To the McDonald brothers, it looked like a way to make money without having to open another restaurant themselves. In 1952, they tried it, but their effort was a dismal failure. The reason was simple: They lacked the leadership necessary to make it effective.

Dick and Maurice were good restaurant owners. They understood how to run a business, make their systems efficient, cut costs, and increase profits. They were efficient managers. But they were not leaders. Their thinking patterns clamped a lid down on what they could do and become. At the height of their success, Dick and Maurice found themselves smack-dab against the Law of the Lid.

THE BROTHERS PARTNER WITH A LEADER

In 1954, the brothers hooked up with a man named Ray Kroc who *was* a leader. Kroc had been running a small company he founded, which sold machines for making milk shakes. McDonald's was one of his best customers, and as soon as he visited the store, he had a vision for its potential. In his mind he could see the restaurant going nationwide in hundreds of markets. He soon struck a deal with Dick and Maurice, and in 1955, he formed McDonald's System, Inc. (later called the McDonald's Corporation).

Kroc immediately bought the rights to a franchise so that he could use it as a model and prototype to sell other franchises. Then he began to assemble a team and build an organization to make McDonald's a nationwide entity.

In the early years, Kroc sacrificed a lot. Though he was in his midfifties, he worked long hours just as he had when he first got started in business thirty years earlier. He eliminated many frills at home, including his country club membership, which he later said added ten strokes to his golf game. During his first eight years with McDonald's, he took no salary. He also personally borrowed money from the bank and against his life insurance to help cover the salaries of a few key leaders he wanted on the team. His sacrifice and his leadership paid off. In 1961 for the sum of $2.7 million, Kroc bought the exclusive rights to McDonald's from the brothers, and he proceeded to turn it into an American institution and global entity. The "lid" in the life and leadership of Ray Kroc was obviously much higher than that of his predecessors.

In the years that Dick and Maurice McDonald had attempted to franchise their food service system, they managed to sell the concept to just fifteen buyers, only ten of whom actually opened restaurants. On the other hand, the leadership lid in Ray Kroc's life was sky high. Between 1955 and 1959, Kroc succeeded in opening 100 restaurants. Four years after that, there were 500 McDonald's. Today the company has opened more than 21,000 restaurants in no fewer than 100 countries.[1] Leadership ability— or more specifically the lack of leadership ability—was the lid on the McDonald brothers' effectiveness.

SUCCESS WITHOUT LEADERSHIP

I believe that success is within the reach of just about everyone. But I also believe that personal success without leadership ability brings only limited effectiveness. A person's impact is only a fraction of what it could be with good leadership. The higher you want to climb, the more you need leadership. The greater the impact you want to make, the greater your influence needs to be. Whatever you will accomplish is restricted by your ability to lead others.

Let me give you a picture of what I mean. Let's say that when it comes to success, you're an 8 (on a scale from 1 to 10). That's pretty good. I think it would be safe to say that the McDonald brothers were in that range. But let's also say that your leadership ability is only a 1. Your level of effectiveness would look like this:

SUCCESS WITHOUT LEADERSHIP

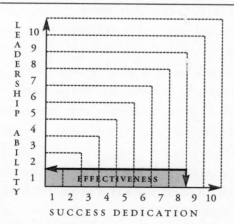

To increase your level of effectiveness, you have a couple of choices. You could work very hard to increase your dedication to success and excellence—to work toward becoming a 10. It's possible that you could make it to that level, though the law of diminishing returns says that your success will increase only to a certain point, after which, it fails to increase in proportion to the amount of work you put into it. In other words, the effort it would take to increase those last two points might take more energy than it did to achieve the first eight. If you really killed yourself, you might increase your success by that 25 percent.

But you have another option. Let's say that instead you work hard to increase your level of *leadership*. Over the course of time, you develop yourself as a leader, and eventually, your leadership ability becomes, say, a 6. Visually, the results would look like the chart on the opposite page.

By raising your leadership ability—without increasing your success dedication at all—you can increase your original effectiveness by 500 percent! If you were to raise your leadership to 8, where it matched your success dedication, you would increase your effectiveness by 700 percent! Leadership has a multiplying effect. I've seen its impact over and over again in all kinds of businesses and nonprofit organizations. And that's why I've taught leadership for more than twenty-five years.

SUCCESS WITH LEADERSHIP

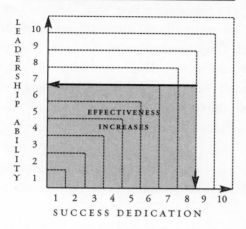

TO CHANGE THE DIRECTION OF THE ORGANIZATION, CHANGE THE LEADER

Leadership ability is always the lid on personal and organizational effectiveness. If the leadership is strong, the lid is high. But if it's not, then the organization is limited. That's why in times of trouble, organizations naturally look for new leadership. When the country is experiencing hard times, it elects a new president. When a church is floundering, it searches for a new senior pastor. When a sports team keeps losing, it looks for a new head coach. When a company is losing money, it hires a new CEO.

A few years ago, I met Don Stephenson, the chairman of Global Hospitality Resources, Inc., of San Diego, California, an international hospitality advisory and consulting firm. Over lunch, I asked him about his organization. Today he primarily does consulting, but back then his company took over the management of hotels and resorts that weren't doing well financially. They oversaw many excellent facilities such as La Costa in southern California.

TO REACH THE HIGHEST LEVEL OF EFFECTIVENESS, YOU
HAVE TO RAISE THE LID OF LEADERSHIP ABILITY.

Don said that whenever they came into an organization to take it over, they always started by doing two things: First, they trained all the staff to improve their level of service to the customers, and second, they fired the leader. When he told me that, I was at first surprised.

"You *always* fire him?" I asked. "Every time?"

"That's right. Every time," he said.

"Don't you talk to the person first—to check him out to see if he's a good leader?" I said.

"No," he answered. "If he'd been a good leader, the organization wouldn't be in the mess it's in."

And I thought to myself, *Of course. It's the Law of the Lid.* To reach the highest level of effectiveness, you have to raise the lid—one way or another.

The good news is that getting rid of the leader isn't the *only* way. Just as I teach in conferences that there is a lid, I also teach that you can raise it.

2

How Can I Grow as a Leader?

*Leadership develops daily,
not in a day.*

Becoming a leader is a lot like investing successfully in the stock market. If your hope is to make a fortune in a day, you're not going to be successful. What matters most is what you do day by day over the long haul. My friend Tag Short maintains, "The secret of our success is found in our daily agenda." If you continually invest in your leadership development, letting your "assets" compound, the inevitable result is growth over time.

When I teach leadership at conferences, people inevitably ask me whether leaders are born. I always answer, "Yes, of course they are . . . I've yet to meet one that came into the world any other way!" We all laugh, and then I answer the real question—whether leadership is something a person either possesses or doesn't.

Although it's true that some people are born with greater

natural gifts than others, the ability to lead is really a collection of skills, nearly all of which can be learned and improved. But that process doesn't happen overnight. Leadership is complicated. It has many facets: respect, experience, emotional strength, people skills, discipline, vision, momentum, timing—the list goes on. As you can see, many factors that come into play in leadership are intangible. That's why leaders require so much seasoning to be effective. It was around the time I turned fifty that I truly began to understand the many aspects of leadership with clarity.

The Four Phases of Leadership Growth

Whether you do or don't have great natural ability for leadership, your development and progress will probably occur according to the following four phases:

Phase 1—I Don't Know What I Don't Know

Most people fail to recognize the value of leadership. They believe that leadership is only for a few—for the people at the top of the corporate ladder. They have no idea of the opportunities they're passing up when they don't learn to lead. This point was driven home for me when a college president shared with me that only a handful of students signed up for a leadership course offered by the school. Why? Only a few thought of themselves as leaders. If they had known that leadership is influence, and that in the course of each day most individuals usually try to influence at least four other people, their desire might have been sparked to learn more about the subject. It's unfortunate because as long as a person doesn't know what he doesn't know, he doesn't grow.

PHASE 2—I KNOW WHAT I DON'T KNOW

Usually at some point in life, we are placed in a leadership position only to look around and discover that no one is following us. That's when we realize that we need to *learn* how to lead. And of course, that's when it's possible for the process to start. English Prime Minister Benjamin Disraeli wisely commented, "To be conscious that you are ignorant of the facts is a great step to knowledge."

SUCCESSFUL LEADERS ARE LEARNERS. AND THE
LEARNING PROCESS IS ONGOING, A RESULT OF
SELF-DISCIPLINE AND PERSEVERANCE.

That's what happened to me when I took my first leadership position in 1969. I had captained sports teams all my life and had been the student government president in college, so I already thought I was a leader. But when I tried to lead people in the real world, I found out the awful truth. That prompted me to start gathering resources and learning from them. I also had another idea: I wrote to the top ten leaders in my field and offered them one hundred dollars for a half hour of their time so that I could ask them questions. (That was quite a sum for me in 1969.) For the next several years, my wife, Margaret, and I planned every vacation around where those people lived. If a great leader in Cleveland said yes to my request, then that year we vacationed in Cleveland so that I could meet him. And my idea really paid off. Those men shared insights with me that I could have learned no other way.

Phase 3—I Grow and Know and It Starts to Show

When you recognize your lack of skill and begin the daily discipline of personal growth in leadership, exciting things start to happen.

Awhile back I was teaching a group of people in Denver, and in the crowd I noticed a really sharp nineteen-year-old named Brian. For a couple of days, I watched as he eagerly took notes. I talked to him a few times during breaks. When I got to the part of the seminar where I emphasize that leadership is a process, I asked Brian to stand up so that I could talk while everyone listened. I said, "Brian, I've been watching you here, and I'm very impressed with how hungry you are to learn and glean and grow. I want to tell you a secret that will change your life." Everyone in the whole auditorium seemed to lean forward.

"I believe that in about twenty years, you can be a *great* leader. I want to encourage you to make yourself a lifelong learner of leadership. Read books, listen to tapes regularly, and keep attending seminars. And whenever you come across a golden nugget of truth or a significant quote, file it away for the future.

"It's not going to be easy," I said. "But in five years, you'll see progress as your influence becomes greater. In ten years you'll develop a competence that makes your leadership highly effective. And in twenty years, when you're only thirty-nine years old, if you've continued to learn and grow, others will likely start asking you to teach them about leadership. And some will be amazed. They'll look at each other and say, 'How did he suddenly become so wise?'

"Brian, you can be a great leader, but it won't happen in a day. Start paying the price now."

What's true for Brian is also true for you. Start developing your leadership today, and someday you will experience the effects of this process.

Phase 4—I Simply Go Because of What I Know

When you're in phase 3, you can be pretty effective as a leader, but you have to think about every move you make. However, when you get to phase 4, your ability to lead becomes almost automatic. And that's when the payoff is larger than life. But the only way to get there is to recognize the process and pay the price.

To Lead Tomorrow, Learn Today

Leadership is developed daily, not in a day—that is reality. The good news is that your leadership ability is not static. No matter where you're starting from, you can get better. That's true even for people who have stood on the world stage of leadership. While most presidents of the United States reach their peak while in office, others continue to grow and become better leaders afterward, such as former president Jimmy Carter. Some people questioned his ability to lead while in the White House. But in recent years, Carter's level of influence has continually increased. His high integrity and dedication in serving people through Habitat for Humanity and other organizations have made his influence grow. People are now truly impressed with his life.

FIGHTING YOUR WAY UP

There is an old saying: Champions don't become champions in the ring—they are merely recognized there. That's true. If you want to see where someone develops into a champion, look at his daily routine. Former heavyweight champ Joe Frazier stated, "You can map out a fight plan or a life plan. But when the action starts, you're down to your reflexes. That's where your road work shows. If you cheated on that in the dark of the morning, you're getting found out now under the bright lights."[1] Boxing is a good analogy for leadership development because it is all about daily preparation. Even if a person has natural talent, he has to prepare and train to become successful.

One of this country's greatest leaders was a fan of boxing: President Theodore Roosevelt. In fact, one of his most famous quotes uses a boxing analogy:

It is not the critic who counts, not the man who points out how the strong man stumbled, or where the doer of deeds could have done them better. The credit belongs to the man who is actually in the arena; whose face is marred by dust and sweat and blood; who strives valiantly; who errs and comes short again and again; who knows the great enthusiasms, the great devotions, and spends himself in a worthy cause; who, at best, knows in the end the triumph of high achievement; and who, at the worst, if he fails, at least fails while daring greatly, so that his place shall never be with those cold and timid souls who know neither victory nor defeat.

A boxer himself, Roosevelt was not only an effective leader, but he was the most flamboyant of all U.S. presidents.

A Man of Action

TR (which was Roosevelt's nickname) was known for regular boxing and judo sessions, challenging horseback rides, and long, strenuous hikes. A French ambassador who visited Roosevelt used to tell about the time that he accompanied the president on a walk through the woods. When the two men came to the banks of a stream that was too deep to cross by foot, TR stripped off his clothes and expected the dignitary to do the same so that they could swim to the other side. Nothing was an obstacle to Roosevelt.

His enthusiasm and stamina seemed boundless. As the vice presidential candidate in 1900, he gave 673 speeches and traveled 20,000 miles while campaigning for President

McKinley. And years after his presidency, while preparing to deliver a speech in Milwaukee, Roosevelt was shot in the chest by a would-be assassin. With a broken rib and a bullet in his chest, Roosevelt insisted on delivering his one-hour speech before allowing himself to be taken to the hospital.

ROOSEVELT STARTED SLOW

Of all the leaders this nation has ever had, Roosevelt was one of the toughest—both physically and mentally. But he didn't start that way. America's cowboy president was born in Manhattan to a prominent wealthy family. As a child, he was puny and very sickly. He had debilitating asthma, possessed very poor eyesight, and was painfully thin. His parents weren't sure he would survive.

When he was twelve, young Roosevelt's father told him, "You have the mind, but you have not the body, and without the help of the body the mind cannot go as far as it should. You must *make* the body." And make it he did. TR began spending time *every day* building his body as well as his mind, and he did that for the rest of his life. He worked out with weights, hiked, ice-skated, hunted, rowed, rode horseback, and boxed. By the time TR graduated from Harvard, he was ready to tackle the world of politics.

No Overnight Success

Roosevelt didn't become a great leader overnight, either. His road to the presidency was one of slow, continual growth. As he served in various positions, ranging from New York City Police Commissioner to President of the United States, he kept learning and growing. He improved himself, and in time he became a strong leader.

Roosevelt's list of accomplishments is remarkable. Under his leadership, the United States emerged as a world power. He helped the country develop a first-class navy. He saw that the Panama Canal was built. He negotiated peace between Russia and Japan, winning a Nobel Peace Prize in the process. And when people questioned TR's leadership—since he had become president when McKinley was assassinated—he campaigned and was reelected by the largest majority of any president up to his time.

Ever the man of action, when Roosevelt completed his term as president in 1909, he immediately traveled to Africa where he led a scientific expedition sponsored by the Smithsonian Institution.

On January 6, 1919, at his home in New York, Theodore Roosevelt died in his sleep. Then Vice President Marshall said, "Death had to take him sleeping, for if Roosevelt had been awake, there would have been a fight." When they removed him from his bed, they found a book under his pillow. Up to the very last, TR was still striving to learn and improve himself.

If you want to be a leader, the good news is that you can do it. Everyone has the potential, but it isn't accomplished overnight. It requires perseverance. And you absolutely cannot ignore that becoming a leader is a process. Leadership doesn't develop in a day. It takes a lifetime.

PART 2

THE TRAITS OF A LEADER

3

How Can I Become Disciplined?

The first person you lead is you.

It's a tough road to the top. Not many people ever reach the place where they are considered one of the best at their work. And even fewer are believed to be *the* best—ever. Yet that's what Jerry Rice has achieved. He is called the best person ever to play wide receiver in football. And he has got the records to prove it.

People who know him well say he is a natural. Physically his God-given gifts are incredible, yet those alone have not made him great. The real key to his success has been his self-discipline. He works and prepares—day in and day out—unlike anyone else in professional football.

During practice in high school, Rice's coach, Charles Davis, made his players sprint twenty times up and down a forty-yard hill. On a particularly hot and muggy Mississippi day, Rice was ready to give up after eleven trips. As he sneaked toward the locker room, he realized what he was doing.

"Don't quit," he told himself. "Because once you get into that mode of quitting, then you feel like it's okay." He went back and finished his sprints, and he has never been a quitter since.

As a professional player, he has become famous for his ability to sprint up another hill—a rugged 2.5-mile park trail in San Carlos, California—that Rice makes a regular part of his workout schedule. Other top players try to keep up with him on it, but they fall behind, astounded by his stamina. But that's only a part of Rice's regular routine. Even in the off-season, while other players are fishing or lying around enjoying downtime, Rice is working, his normal exercise routine lasting from 7:00 A.M. to noon. Someone once joked, "He is so well-conditioned that he makes Jamie Lee Curtis look like James Earl Jones."

"What a lot of guys don't understand about Jerry is that with him, football's a twelve-month thing," says NFL cornerback Kevin Smith. "He's a natural, but he still works. That's what separates the good from the great."

NO MATTER HOW GIFTED A LEADER IS, HIS GIFTS WILL NEVER
REACH THEIR MAXIMUM POTENTIAL WITHOUT
THE APPLICATION OF SELF-DISCIPLINE.

In 1997, Rice climbed another hill in his career: he made a comeback from a devastating injury. Prior to that, he had never missed a game in nineteen seasons of football, a testament to his disciplined work ethic and absolute tenacity. When he blew out his knee on August 31, 1997, people thought he was finished for the season. After all, only one player had ever had a similar injury and come back in the same season—Rod Woodson. He had rehabilitated his knee in four and a half months. Rice did it in three and a half—through sheer grit, determination, and incredible self- discipline. People had never seen anything like it before, and they might not again. And Rice continues to build his records and his reputation while helping his team win.

A Disciplined Direction

Jerry Rice is a perfect example of the power of self-discipline. No one achieves and sustains success without it. And no matter how gifted a leader is, his gifts will never reach their maximum potential without the application of self-discipline. It positions a leader to go to the highest level and is a key to leadership that lasts.

If you want to become a leader for whom self-discipline is an asset, follow these action points:

Challenge Your Excuses

To develop a lifestyle of discipline, one of your first tasks must be to challenge and eliminate any tendency to make excuses. As French classical writer François La Rochefoucauld said, "Almost all our faults are more pardonable than the methods we think up to hide them." If you have several reasons why you can't be self-disciplined, realize that they are really just a bunch of excuses—all of which need to be challenged if you want to go to the next level as a leader.

REMOVE REWARDS UNTIL THE JOB IS DONE

Author Mike Delaney wisely remarked, "Any business or industry that pays equal rewards to its goof-offs and its eager-beavers sooner or later will find itself with more goof-offs than eager-beavers." If you lack self-discipline, you may be in the habit of having dessert before eating your vegetables.

A story illustrates the power of withholding rewards. An older couple had been at a campground for a couple of days when a family arrived at the site next to them. As soon as their sport-utility vehicle came to a stop, the couple and their three kids piled out. One child hurriedly unloaded ice chests, backpacks, and other items while the other two quickly put up tents. The site was ready in fifteen minutes.

The older couple was amazed. "You folks sure do work great together," the elderly gentleman told the dad admiringly.

"You just need a system," replied the dad. "Nobody goes to the bathroom until camp's set up."

Stay Focused on Results

Anytime you concentrate on the difficulty of the work instead of its results or rewards, you're likely to become discouraged. Dwell on it too long, and you'll develop self-pity instead of self-discipline. The next time you're facing a must-do task and you're thinking of doing what's convenient instead of paying the price, change your focus. Count the benefits of doing what's right, and then dive in.

IF YOU KNOW YOU HAVE TALENT, AND YOU'VE SEEN A
LOT OF MOTION BUT LITTLE CONCRETE RESULTS—
YOU MAY LACK SELF-DISCIPLINE.

Author H. Jackson Brown Jr. quipped, "Talent without discipline is like an octopus on roller skates. There's plenty of movement, but you never know if it's going to be forward, backwards, or sideways." If you know you have talent, and you've seen a lot of motion—but little concrete results—you may lack self-discipline.

Look at last week's schedule. How much of your time did you devote to regular, disciplined activities? Did you do anything to grow and improve yourself professionally? Did you engage in activities promoting good health? Did you dedicate part of your income to savings or investments? If you've been putting off those things, telling yourself that you'll do them later, you may need to work on your self-discipline.

4

HOW SHOULD I PRIORITIZE MY LIFE?

*The discipline to prioritize and the ability
to work toward a stated goal are essential
to a leader's success.*

S uccess can be defined as *the progressive realization of a
predetermined goal.* This definition tells us that the discipline to prioritize and the ability to work toward a stated goal are essential to a leader's success. In fact, I believe they are the key to leadership.

Many years ago, while working toward a business degree, I learned about the Pareto Principle. It is commonly called the 20/80 principle. Although I received little information about this principle at the time, I began applying it to my life. Years later I find it is a most useful tool for determining priorities for any person's life or for any organization.

THE PARETO PRINCIPLE: THE 20/80 PRINCIPLE

Twenty percent of your priorities will give you 80 percent of your production, IF you spend your time, energy, money, and personnel on the top 20 percent of your priorities.

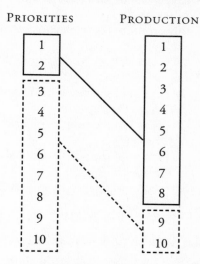

The solid lines on the illustration of the 20/80 Principle above represent a person or organization that spends time, energy, money, and personnel on the most important priorities. The result is a four-fold return in productivity. The dotted lines represent a person or organization that spends time, energy, money, and personnel on the lesser priorities. The result is a very small return.

Examples of the Pareto Principle:

Time	20 percent of our time produces 80 percent of the results.
Counseling	20 percent of the people take up 80 percent of our time.
Products	20 percent of the products bring in 80 percent of the profit.
Reading	20 percent of the book contains 80 percent of the content.
Job	20 percent of our work gives us 80 percent of our satisfaction.
Speech	20 percent of the presentation produces 80 percent of the impact.
Donations	20 percent of the people will give 80 percent of the money.
Leadership	20 percent of the people will make 80 percent of the decisions.
Picnic	20 percent of the people will eat 80 percent of the food!

Every leader needs to understand the Pareto Principle in the area of people oversight and leadership. For example, 20 percent of the people in an organization will be responsible for 80 percent of the company's success. The following strategy will enable a leader to increase the productivity of an organization.

1. Determine which people are the top 20 percent producers.

2. Spend 80 percent of your "people time" with the top 20 percent.
3. Spend 80 percent of your personal development dollars on the top 20 percent.
4. Determine what 20 percent of the work gives 80 percent of the return and train an assistant to do the 80 percent less-effective work. This "frees up" the producer to do what he/she does best.
5. Ask the top 20 percent to do on-the-job training for the next 20 percent.

Remember, we teach what we know; we reproduce what we are. Like begets like. I teach this principle at leadership conferences, and I am often asked, "How do I identify the top 20 percent influencers/producers in my organization?" I suggest that you make a list of everyone in your company or department. Then ask yourself this question about each individual: "If this person takes a negative action against me or withdraws his or her support from me, what will the impact likely be?" If you won't be able to function, then put a check mark next to that name. If the person can help you or hurt you, but cannot make or break you in terms of your ability to get important things done, then don't put a check mark next to that name. When you get through making the check marks, you will have marked between 15 and 20 percent of the names. Those are the vital relationships that need to be developed and given the proper amount of resources needed to grow the organization.

ORGANIZE OR AGONIZE

Remember: It's not how hard you work; it's how smart you work. The ability to juggle three or four high priority projects successfully is a must for every leader.

A LIFE IN WHICH ANYTHING GOES WILL ULTIMATELY
BE A LIFE IN WHICH NOTHING GOES.

Prioritize Assignments

High Importance/High Urgency: Tackle these projects first.

High Importance/Low Urgency: Set deadlines for completion and get these projects worked into your daily routine.

Low Importance/High Urgency: Find quick, efficient ways to get this work done without much personal involvement. If possible, delegate it to a "can do" assistant.

Low Importance/Low Urgency: This is busy or repetitious work, such as filing. Stack it up and do it in one-half hour segments every week; get somebody else to do it; or don't do it at all. Before putting off until tomorrow something you can do today, study it clearly. Maybe you can postpone it indefinitely.

CHOOSE OR LOSE

Every person is an initiator or reactor when it comes to planning. An example is our calendar. The question is not "Will my calendar be full?" but "Who will fill my calendar?" If we are leaders of others, the question is not "Will I see people?" but "Who will I see?" My observation is that leaders tend to initiate and followers tend to react. Note the difference:

LEADERS	FOLLOWERS
Initiate	React
Lead; pick up phone and make contact	Listen; wait for phone to ring
Spend time planning; anticipate problems	Spend time living day-to-day reacting to problems
Invest time with people	Spend time with people
Fill the calendar by priorities	Fill the calendar by requests

EVALUATE OR STALEMATE

Many times priorities are not black or white, but many tones of gray. I have found that the last thing one knows is what to put first. The following questions will assist your priority process:

What is required of me? A leader can give up anything except final responsibility. The question that must always be answered before accepting a new job is "What is required of me?" In other words, what do I have to do that no one but me can do? Whatever those things are, they must be put high on the priority list. Failure to do them will cause you to be among the unemployed. There will be many responsibilities of the levels under your position, but only a few that require you to be the one and only one who can do them. Distinguish between what you have to do and what can be delegated to someone else.

What gives me the greatest return? The effort expended should approximate the results expected. A question I must continually ask myself is, "Am I doing what I do best and receiving a good return for the organization?" Three common problems in many organizations are:

- Abuse: Too few employees are doing too much.
- Disuse: Too many employees are doing too little.
- Misuse: Too many employees are doing the wrong things.

What is most rewarding? Life is too short not to be fun. Our best work takes place when we enjoy it. Some time ago I spoke at a leaders' conference where I attempted to teach this principle. The title of my lecture was "Take This Job and Love It." I encouraged the audience to find something they liked to do so much they would gladly do it for nothing. Then I suggested they learn to do it so well that people would be happy to pay them for it. You enjoy yourself because you are making your contribution to the world.

Success in your work will be greatly increased if the three Rs—Requirements, Return, Reward—are similar. In other words, if the requirements of my job are the same as my strengths that give me the highest return and doing those things brings me great pleasure, then I will be successful if I act on my priorities.

PRIORITY PRINCIPLES

PRIORITIES NEVER "STAY PUT"

Priorities continually shift and demand attention. H. Ross Perot said that anything that is excellent or praiseworthy stands moment-by-moment on the cutting edge and must be constantly fought for. Well-placed priorities always sit on "the edge."

To keep priorities in place:

- Evaluate: Every month review the three Rs (Requirements/Return/Reward).
- Eliminate: Ask yourself, "What am I doing that can be done by someone else?"
- Estimate: What are the top projects you are doing this month and how long will they take?

YOU CANNOT OVERESTIMATE THE
UNIMPORTANCE OF PRACTICALLY EVERYTHING

I love this principle. It's a little exaggerated but needs to be said. William James said that the art of being wise is "the art of knowing what to overlook." The petty and the mundane steal much of our time. Too many are living for the wrong things.

Dr. Anthony Campolo tells about a sociological study in which fifty people over the age of ninety-five were asked one question: "If you could live your life over again, what would you do differently?" It was an open-ended question, and a multiplicity of answers came from these eldest of senior citizens. However, three answers constantly reemerged and dominated the results of the study. Those answers were:

- If I had it to do over again, I would reflect more.
- If I had it to do over again, I would risk more.
- If I had it to do over again, I would do more things that would live on after I am dead.

A young concert violinist was asked the secret of her success. She replied, "Planned neglect." Then she explained, "When I was in school, there were many things that demanded my time. When I went to my room after breakfast, I made my bed, straightened the room, dusted the floor, and did whatever else came to my attention. Then I hurried to my violin practice. I found I wasn't progressing as I thought I should, so I reversed things. Until my practice period was completed, I deliberately neglected everything else. That program of planned neglect, I believe, accounts for my success."[1]

THE GOOD IS THE ENEMY OF THE BEST

Most people can prioritize when faced with right or wrong issues. The challenge arises when we are faced with two good choices. Now what should we do? What if both choices fall comfortably into the requirements, return, and reward of our work?

How to Break the Tie Between Two Good Options

- Ask your overseer or coworkers their preference.
- Can one of the options be handled by someone else? If so, pass it on and work on the one only you can do.
- Which option would be of more benefit to the customer? Too many times we are like the merchant who was so intent on trying to keep the store clean that he would never unlock the front door. The real reason for running the store is to have customers come in, not to clean it up!
- Make your decision based on the purpose of the organization.

TOO MANY PRIORITIES PARALYZE US

Every one of us has looked at our desks filled with memos and papers, heard the phone ringing, and watched the door open all at the same time! Remember the "frozen feeling" that came over you?

William H. Hinson tells us why animal trainers carry a stool when they go into a cage of lions. They have their whips, of course, and their pistols are at their sides. But invariably they also carry a stool. Hinson says it is the most important tool of the trainer. He holds the stool by the back and thrusts the legs toward the face of the wild animal. Those who know maintain that the animal tries to focus on all four legs at once. In the attempt to focus on all four, a kind of paralysis overwhelms the animal, and it becomes tame, weak, and disabled because its attention is fragmented. (Now we will have more empathy for the lions.)

If you are overloaded with work, list the priorities on a separate sheet of paper *before* you take it to your boss and see what he will choose as the priorities.

The last of each month I plan and lay out my priorities for the next month. I sit down with my assistant and have her place those projects on the calendar. She handles hundreds of things for me on a monthly basis. However, when something is of High Importance/High Urgency, I communicate that to her so it will be placed above other things.

All true leaders have learned to say no to the good in order to say yes to the best.

When Little Priorities Demand Too Much of Us, Big Problems Arise

Robert J. McKain said, "The reason most major goals are not achieved is that we spend our time doing second things first."

EFFICIENCY IS THE FOUNDATION FOR SURVIVAL.
EFFECTIVENESS IS THE FOUNDATION FOR SUCCESS.

Often the little things in life trip us up. A tragic example is an Eastern Airlines jumbo jet that crashed in the Everglades of Florida. The plane was the now-famous Flight 401, bound from New York to Miami with a heavy load of holiday passengers. As the plane approached the Miami airport for its landing, the light that indicates proper deployment of the landing gear failed to light. The plane flew in a large, looping circle over the swamps of the Everglades while the cockpit crew checked to see if the gear actually had not deployed, or if instead the bulb in the signal light was defective.

When the flight engineer tried to remove the light bulb, it wouldn't budge, and the other members of the crew tried to help him. As they struggled with the bulb, no one noticed the aircraft was losing altitude, and the plane simply flew right into the swamp. Dozens of people were killed in the crash. While an experienced crew of high-priced pilots fiddled with a seventy-five cent light bulb, the plane with its passengers flew right into the ground.

TIME DEADLINES AND EMERGENCIES
FORCE US TO PRIORITIZE

We find this in Parkinson's Law: If you have only one letter to write, it will take all day to do it. If you have twenty letters to write, you'll get them done in one day. When is our most efficient time in our work? The week before vacation! Why can't we always run our lives the way we do the week before we leave the office, making decisions, cleaning off the desk, returning calls? Under normal conditions, we are efficient (doing things right). When time pressure mounts or emergencies arise, we become effective (doing the right things). Efficiency is the foundation for survival. Effectiveness is the foundation of success.

On the night of April 14, 1912, the great ocean liner, the *Titanic*, crashed into an iceberg in the Atlantic and sank, causing great loss of life. One of the most curious stories to come from the disaster was of a woman who had a place in one of the lifeboats.

She asked if she could return to her stateroom for something and was given just three minutes. In her stateroom she ignored her own jewelry, and instead grabbed three oranges. Then she quickly returned to her place in the boat.

Just hours earlier it would have been ludicrous to think she would have accepted a crate of oranges in exchange for even one small diamond, but circumstances had suddenly transformed all the values aboard the ship. The emergency had clarified her priorities.

Too Often We Learn Too Late
What Is Really Important

Gary Redding tells this story about Senator Paul Tsongas of Massachusetts. In January 1984 he announced that he would retire from the U.S. Senate and not seek reelection. Tsongas was a rising political star. He was a strong favorite to be reelected, and had even been mentioned as a potential future candidate for the Presidency or Vice Presidency of the United States.

A few weeks before his announcement, Tsongas had learned he had a form of lymphatic cancer which could not be cured but could be treated. In all likelihood, it would not greatly affect his physical abilities or life expectancy. The illness did not force Tsongas out of the Senate, but it did force him to face the reality of his own mortality. He would not be able to do everything he might want to do. So what were the things he really wanted to do in the time he had?

He decided that what he wanted most in life, what he would not give up if he could not have everything, was being with his family and watching his children grow up. He would rather do that than shape the nation's laws or get his name in the history books.

Shortly after his decision was announced, a friend wrote a note to congratulate Tsongas on having his priorities straight. The note read: "Nobody on his deathbed ever said, 'I wish I had spent more time on my business.'"

5

HOW DO I DEVELOP TRUST?

Trust is the foundation of leadership.

One of the most important lessons a leader can learn is how trust works. To me, it is a little like earning and spending pocket change. Each time you make a good leadership decision, it puts change into your pocket. Each time you make a poor one, you have to pay out some of your change to the people.

Every leader has a certain amount of change in his pocket when he starts in a new leadership position. From then on, he either builds up his change or pays it out. If he makes one bad decision after another, he keeps paying out change. Then one day, after making one last bad decision, he is going to reach into his pocket and realize he is out of change. It doesn't even matter if the blunder was big or small. When you're out of change, you're out as a leader.

A leader's history of successes and failures makes a big difference in his credibility. Your people know when you make

357

mistakes. The real question is whether you're going to 'fess up. If you do, you can often quickly regain their trust. I've learned firsthand that when it comes to leadership, you just can't take shortcuts, no matter how long you've been leading your people.

TRUST IS THE FOUNDATION OF LEADERSHIP

There are three qualities a leader must exemplify to build trust: competence, connection, and character. People will forgive occasional mistakes based on ability, especially if they can see that you're still growing as a leader. But they won't trust someone who has slips in character. In that area, even occasional lapses are lethal. All effective leaders know this truth. PepsiCo chairman and CEO Craig Weatherup acknowledges, "People will tolerate honest mistakes, but if you violate their trust you will find it very difficult to ever regain their confidence. That is one reason that you need to treat trust as your most precious asset. You may fool your boss but you can never fool your colleagues or subordinates."

General H. Norman Schwarzkopf points to the significance of character: "Leadership is a potent combination of strategy and character. But if you must be without one, be without strategy." Character and leadership credibility always go hand in hand. Anthony Harrigan, president of the U.S. Business and Industrial Council, said,

> The role of character always has been the key factor in the rise and fall of nations. And one can be sure that America is no exception to this rule of history. We won't survive as a country because we are smarter or more sophisticated but because we are—we hope—stronger inwardly. In short, character is the only effective bulwark against internal and external forces that lead to a country's disintegration or collapse.

Character makes trust possible. And trust makes leadership possible.

CHARACTER COMMUNICATES

Character communicates many things to followers:

CHARACTER COMMUNICATES CONSISTENCY

Leaders without inner strength can't be counted on day after day because their ability to perform changes constantly. NBA great Jerry West commented, "You can't get too much done in life if you only work on the days when you feel good." If your people don't know what to expect from you as a leader, at some point they won't look to you for leadership.

WHEN A LEADER'S CHARACTER IS STRONG, PEOPLE
TRUST HIM, AND THEY TRUST IN HIS ABILITY
TO RELEASE THEIR POTENTIAL.

Think about what happened in the late 1980s. Several high-profile Christian leaders stumbled and fell due to moral issues. That lack of consistency compromised their ability to lead their people. In fact, it gave a black eye to every pastor across the nation because it caused people to become suspicious of all church leaders, regardless of their personal track records. The flawed character of those fallen leaders destroyed the foundation for their leadership.

When I think of leaders who epitomize consistency of character, the first person who comes to mind is Billy Graham. Regardless of personal religious beliefs, everybody trusts him. Why? Because he has modeled high character for more than half a century. He lives out his values every day. He never makes a commitment unless he is going to keep it. And he goes out of his way to personify integrity.

CHARACTER COMMUNICATES POTENTIAL

John Morley observed, "No man can climb out beyond the limitations of his own character." That's especially true when it comes to leadership. Take, for instance, the case of NHL coach Mike Keenan. As of mid-1997, he had a noteworthy record of professional hockey victories: the fifth greatest number of regular-season wins, the third greatest number of play-off victories, six division titles, four NHL finals appearances, and one Stanley Cup.

Yet despite those commendable credentials, Keenan was unable to stay with a single team for any length of time. In eleven and a half seasons, he coached four different teams. And after his stint with the fourth team—the St. Louis Blues—he was unable to land a job for a long time. Why? Sportswriter E. M. Swift said of Keenan, "The reluctance to hire Keenan is *easily* explicable. Everywhere he has been, he has alienated players and management."[1] Evidently, his players didn't trust him. Neither did the owners, who were benefiting from seeing their teams win.

Craig Weatherup explains, "You don't build trust by talking about it. You build it by achieving results, always with integrity and in a manner that shows real personal regard for the people with whom you work."[2] When a leader's character is strong, people trust him, and they trust in his ability to release their potential. That not only gives followers hope for the future, but it also promotes a strong belief in themselves and their organization.

CHARACTER COMMUNICATES RESPECT

When you don't have strength within, you can't earn respect without. And respect is absolutely essential for lasting leadership. How do leaders earn respect? By making sound decisions, admitting their mistakes, and putting what's best for their followers and the organization ahead of their personal agendas.

A leader's good character builds trust among his followers. But when a leader breaks trust, he forfeits his ability to lead. I was again reminded of this while listening to a lesson taught by my friend Bill Hybels. Four times a year, he and I teach a seminar called "Leading and Communicating to Change Lives." Bill was conducting a session titled "Lessons from a Leadership Nightmare," and he shared observations and insights on some of the leadership mistakes made by Robert McNamara and the Johnson administration during the Vietnam War: the administration's inability to prioritize multiple challenges, its acceptance of faulty assumptions, and Johnson's failure to face serious staff conflicts. But in my opinion, the greatest insight Bill shared during that talk concerned the failure of American leaders, including McNamara, to face and publicly admit the terrible mistakes they had made concerning the war in Vietnam. Their actions broke trust with the American people, and the United States has been suffering from the repercussions ever since.

No leader can break trust with his people and expect to keep the same level of influence with them. Trust is the foundation of leadership. Violate your people's trust, and you're through as a leader.

6

HOW CAN I EFFECTIVELY CAST VISION?

You can seize only what you can see.

One of the great dreamers of the twentieth century was Walt Disney. Any person who could create the first sound cartoon, first all-color cartoon, and first animated feature-length motion picture is definitely someone with vision. But Disney's greatest masterpieces of vision were Disneyland and Walt Disney World. And the spark for that vision came from an unexpected place.

Back when Walt's two daughters were young, he took them to an amusement park in the Los Angeles area on Saturday mornings. His girls loved it, and he did too. An amusement park is a kid's paradise, with wonderful atmosphere.

Walt was especially captivated by the carousel. As he approached it, he saw a blur of bright images racing around to the tune of energetic calliope music. But when he got closer and the carousel stopped, he could see that his eye had been fooled. He observed shabby horses with cracked and chipped paint. And he noticed that only the horses on the outside row moved up and down. The others stood lifeless, bolted to the floor.

The cartoonist's disappointment inspired him with a grand vision. In his mind's eye he could see an amusement park where the illusion didn't evaporate, where children and adults could enjoy a carnival atmosphere without the seedy side that accompanies some circuses or traveling carnivals. His dream became Disneyland. As Larry Taylor stated in *Be an Orange,* Walt's vision could be summarized as, "No chipped paint. All the horses jump."

LOOK BEFORE YOU LEAD

Vision is everything for a leader. It is utterly indispensable. Why? Because vision leads the leader. It paints the target. It sparks and fuels the fire within, and draws him forward. It is also the fire lighter for others who follow that leader. Show me a leader without vision, and I'll show you someone who isn't going anywhere. At best, he is traveling in circles.

To get a handle on vision and how it comes to be a part of a good leader's life, understand these things:

VISION STARTS WITHIN

When I'm teaching at conferences, someone will occasionally ask me to give him a vision for his organization.

But I can't do it. You can't buy, beg, or borrow vision. It has to come from the inside. For Disney, vision was never a problem. Because of his creativity and desire for excellence, he always saw what *could* be.

If you lack vision, look inside yourself. Draw on your natural gifts and desires. Look to your calling if you have one. And if you still don't sense a vision of your own, then consider hooking up with a leader whose vision resonates with you. Become his partner. That's what Walt Disney's brother, Roy, did. He was a good businessman and leader who could make things happen, but Walt provided the vision. Together, they made an incredible team.

VISION DRAWS ON YOUR HISTORY

Vision isn't some mystical quality that comes out of a vacuum, as some people seem to believe. It grows from a leader's past and the history of the people around him. That was the case for Disney. But it's true for all leaders. Talk to any leader, and you're likely to discover key events in his past that were instrumental in the creation of his vision.

VISION MEETS OTHERS' NEEDS

True vision is far-reaching. It goes beyond what one individual can accomplish. And if it has real value, it does more than just *include* others; it *adds value* to them. If you have a vision that doesn't serve others, it's probably too small.

Vision Helps You Gather Resources

One of the most valuable benefits of vision is that it acts like a magnet—attracting, challenging, and uniting people. It also rallies finances and other resources. The greater the vision, the more winners it has the potential to attract. The more challenging the vision, the harder the participants fight to achieve it. Edwin Land, the founder of Polaroid, advised, "The first thing you do is teach the person to feel that the vision is very important and nearly impossible. That draws out the drive in winners."

Focus on Listening

Where does vision come from? To find the vision that is indispensable to leadership, you have to become a good listener. You must listen to several voices.

The Inner Voice

As I have already said, vision starts within. Do you know your life's mission? What stirs your heart? What do you dream about? If what you're pursuing doesn't come from a desire within—from the very depths of who you are and what you believe—you will not be able to accomplish it.

THE UNHAPPY VOICE

Where does inspiration for great ideas come from? From noticing what *doesn't* work. Discontent with the *status quo* is a great catalyst for vision. Are you on complacent cruise control? Or do you find yourself itching to change your world? No great leader in history has fought to prevent change.

THE SUCCESSFUL VOICE

Nobody can accomplish great things alone. To fulfill a big vision, you need a good team. But you also need good advice from someone who is ahead of you in the leadership journey. If you want to lead others to greatness, find a mentor. Do you have an adviser who can help you sharpen your vision?

THINK ABOUT WHAT YOU'D LIKE TO SEE CHANGE IN THE WORLD AROUND YOU.

THE HIGHER VOICE

Although it's true that your vision must come from within, you shouldn't let it be confined by your limited capabilities. A truly valuable vision must have God in it. Only He knows your full capabilities. Have you looked beyond yourself, even beyond your own lifetime, as you've sought your vision? If not, you may be missing your true potential and life's best for you.

To improve your vision, do the following:

Measure yourself. If you have previously thought about the vision for your life and articulated it, measure how well you are carrying it out. Talk to several key people, such as your spouse, a close friend, and key employees, asking them to state what they think your vision is. If *they* can articulate it, then *you* are probably living it.

Do a gut check. If you haven't done a lot of work on vision, spend the next several weeks or months thinking about it. Consider what really impacts you at a gut level. *What makes you cry? What makes you dream? What gives you energy?*

Also think about what you'd like to see change in the world around you. What do you see that isn't—but could be? Once your ideas start to become clearer, write them down and talk to a mentor about them.

From 1923 to 1955, Robert Woodruff served as president of Coca-Cola. During that time, he wanted Coca-Cola to be available to every American serviceman around the world for five cents, no matter what it cost the company. What a bold goal! But it was nothing compared to the bigger picture he could see in his mind's eye. In his lifetime, he wanted every person in the *world* to have tasted Coca-Cola. When you look deep into your heart and soul for a vision, what do *you* see?

PART 3

THE IMPACT OF A LEADER

WHY IS INFLUENCE IMPORTANT?

*The true measure of leadership is influence—
nothing more, nothing less.*

I f you don't have influence, you will *never* be able to lead others. So how do you find and measure influence? Here's a story to answer that question.

In late summer of 1997, people were jolted by two events that occurred less than a week apart: the deaths of Princess Diana and Mother Teresa. On the surface, the two women could not have been more different. One was a tall, young, glamorous princess from England who circulated in the highest society. The other, a Nobel Peace Prize recipient, was a small, elderly Catholic nun born in Albania, who served the poorest of the poor in Calcutta, India.

What's incredible is that their impact was remarkably similar. In a 1996 poll published by the London *Daily Mail,* Princess Diana and Mother Teresa were voted in first and second places as the world's two most caring people.

That's something that doesn't happen unless you have a lot of influence. How did someone like Diana come to be regarded in the same way as Mother Teresa? The answer is that she demonstrated the power of influence.

DIANA CAPTURED THE WORLD'S IMAGINATION

In 1981, Diana became the most talked-about person on the globe when she married Prince Charles of England. Nearly one billion people watched Diana's wedding ceremony televised from St. Paul's Cathedral. And since that day, it seemed people never could get enough news about her. People were intrigued with Diana, a commoner who had once been a kindergarten teacher. At first she seemed painfully shy and totally overwhelmed by all the attention she and her new husband were receiving. Early in their marriage, some reports stated that Diana wasn't very happy performing the duties expected of her as a royal princess. However, in time she adjusted to her new role. As she started traveling and representing the royal family around the world at various functions, she quickly made it her goal to serve others and raise funds for numerous charitable causes. And during the process, she built many important relationships—with politicians, organizers of humanitarian causes, entertainers, and heads of state.

Diana started rallying people to causes such as medical research for AIDS, care for people with leprosy, and a ban on land mines. She was quite influential in bringing that last issue to the attention of the world's leaders. On a visit to the United States just months before her death, she met with members of the Clinton administration to convince them to support the Oslo conference banning the devices. And a few weeks later, they made changes in their position. Patrick Fuller of the British Red Cross said, "The attention she drew to the issue influenced Clinton. She put the issue on the world agenda, there's no doubt about that."[1]

THE EMERGENCE OF A LEADER

In the beginning, Diana's title had merely given her a platform to address others, but she soon became a person of influence in her own right. In 1996 when she was divorced from Prince Charles, she lost her title, but that loss didn't at all diminish her impact on others. Instead, her influence continued to increase while that of her former husband and in-laws declined—despite their royal titles and position.

Ironically, even in death Diana continued to influence others. When her funeral was broadcast on television and BBC Radio, it was translated into forty-four languages.

NBC estimated that the total audience numbered as many as 2.5 billion people—more than twice the number of people who watched her wedding.

TRUE LEADERSHIP CANNOT BE AWARDED, APPOINTED, OR ASSIGNED. IT COMES ONLY FROM INFLUENCE.

Princess Diana has been characterized in many ways. But one word that I've never heard used to describe her is *leader*. Yet that's what she was. Ultimately, she made things happen because she was an influencer, and leadership is influence—nothing more, nothing less.

FIVE MYTHS ABOUT LEADERSHIP

There are plenty of misconceptions and myths that people embrace about leaders and leadership. Here are five common ones:

I. THE MANAGEMENT MYTH

A widespread misunderstanding is that leading and managing are one and the same. Up until a few years ago, books that claimed to be on leadership were often really about management. The main difference between the two is that leadership is about influencing people to follow, while management focuses on maintaining systems and processes. The best way to test whether a person can lead rather than just manage is to ask him to create positive change. Managers can maintain direction, but they can't change it. To move people in a new direction, you need influence.

2. THE ENTREPRENEUR MYTH

Frequently, people assume that all salespeople and entrepreneurs are leaders. But that's not always the case. You may remember the Ronco commercials that appeared on television years ago. They sold items such as the Veg-O-Matic, Pocket Fisherman, and Inside-the-Shell Egg Scrambler. Those products were the brainchildren of an entrepreneur named Ron Popeil. Called the salesman of the century, he has also appeared in numerous infomercials for products such as spray-on relief for baldness and food dehydrating devices.

Popeil is certainly enterprising, innovative, and successful, especially if you measure him by the $300 million in sales his products have earned. But that doesn't make him a leader. People may be buying what he has to sell, but they're not following him. At best, he is able to persuade people for a moment, but he holds no long-term influence with them.

3. THE KNOWLEDGE MYTH

Sir Francis Bacon said, "Knowledge is power." Most people, believing power is the essence of leadership, naturally assume that those who possess knowledge and intelligence are leaders. But that isn't automatically true. You can visit any major university and meet brilliant research scientists and philosophers whose ability to think is so high that it's off the charts, but whose ability to lead is so low that it doesn't even register on the charts. IQ doesn't necessarily equate to leadership.

4. THE PIONEER MYTH

Another misconception is that anyone who is out in front of the crowd is a leader. But being first isn't always the same as leading. For example, Sir Edmund Hillary was the first man to reach the summit of Mount Everest. Since his historic ascent in 1953, many people have "followed" him in achieving that feat. But that doesn't make Hillary a leader. He wasn't even the leader on that particular expedition. John Hunt was. And when Hillary traveled to the South Pole in 1958 as part of the Commonwealth Trans-Antarctic Expedition, he was accompanying another leader, Sir Vivian Fuchs. To be a leader, a person has to not only be out front, but also have people intentionally coming behind him, following his lead, and acting on his vision.

5. The Position Myth

The greatest misunderstanding about leadership is that people think it is based on position, but it's not. Stanley Huffty affirmed, "It's not the position that makes the leader; it's the leader that makes the position."

Look at what happened several years ago at Cordiant, the advertising agency formerly known as Saatchi & Saatchi. In 1994, institutional investors at Saatchi & Saatchi forced the board of directors to dismiss Maurice Saatchi, the company's CEO. What was the result? Several executives followed him out. So did many of the company's largest accounts, including British Airways and Mars, the candy maker. Saatchi's influence was so great that his departure caused the company's stock to fall immediately from $8⅝ to $4 per share.[2] Saatchi lost his title and position, but he continued to be the leader.

WHO'S THE REAL LEADER?

I personally learned the significance of influence when I accepted my first job out of college at a small church in rural Indiana. I went in with all the right credentials. I was hired as the senior pastor, which meant that I possessed the position and title of leader in that organization. I had the proper college degree. I had even been ordained. In addition, I had been trained by my father who was an excellent pastor and a very high-profile leader in the denomination. It made for a good-looking résumé—but it didn't make me a leader. At my first board meeting, I quickly found out who was the real leader of that church. By the time I took my next position three years later, I had learned the importance of influence. I recognized that hard work was required to gain influence in any organization and to earn the right to become the leader.

LEADERSHIP WITHOUT LEVERAGE

I admire and respect the leadership of my good friend Bill Hybels, the senior pastor of Willow Creek Community Church in South Barrington, Illinois, the largest church in North America. Bill says he believes that the church is the most leadership-intensive enterprise in society. A lot of businesspeople I know are surprised when they hear that statement, but I think Bill is right. What is the basis of his belief? Positional leadership doesn't work in volunteer organizations. If a leader doesn't have leverage—or influence—then he is ineffective. In other organizations, the person who has position has incredible leverage. In the military, leaders can use rank and, if all else fails, throw people into the brig. In business, bosses have tremendous leverage in the form of salary, benefits, and perks. Most followers are pretty cooperative when their livelihood is at stake.

FOLLOWERS IN VOLUNTARY ORGANIZATIONS
CANNOT BE FORCED TO GET ON BOARD.
IF THE LEADER HAS NO INFLUENCE WITH
THEM, THEN THEY WON'T FOLLOW.

But in voluntary organizations, such as churches, the only thing that works is leadership in its purest form. Leaders have only their influence to aid them. And as Harry A. Overstreet observed, "The very essence of all power to influence lies in getting the other person to participate." Followers in voluntary organizations cannot be forced to get on board. If the leader has no influence with them, then they won't follow. If you are a businessperson and you really want to find out whether your people are capable of leading, send them out to volunteer their time in the community. If they can get people to follow them while they're serving at the Red Cross, a United Way shelter, or their local church, then you know that they really do have influence—and leadership ability.

Here is my favorite leadership proverb: "He who thinks he leads, but has no followers, is only taking a walk." If you can't influence others, they won't follow you. And if they won't follow, you're not a leader. No matter what anybody else tells you, remember that leadership is influence—nothing more, nothing less.

How Does Influence Work?

Real leadership is being the person others
will gladly and confidently follow.

Sociologists tell us that even the most introverted individual influences ten thousand other people during his or her lifetime! This amazing statistic was shared with me by my associate Tim Elmore. Tim and I concluded that each one of us is both influencing and being influenced by others.

Influence Can Be Developed

The prominent leader of any group is quite easily discovered. Just observe the people as they gather. If an issue is to be decided, who is the person whose opinion seems most valuable? Who is the one with whom people quickly agree? Most importantly, who is the one the others follow?

Robert Dilenschneider, the CEO of Hill and Knowlton, a worldwide public relations agency, is one of the nation's major influence brokers. He skillfully weaves his persuasive magic in the global arena where governments and mega-corporations meet. He wrote a book entitled *Power and Influence*, in which he shares the idea of the "power triangle" to help leaders get ahead. He says, "The three components of this triangle are communication, recognition, and influence. You start to communicate effectively. This leads to recognition and recognition in turn leads to influence."[1]

THE LEVELS OF LEADERSHIP

We can increase our influence and leadership potential if we understand the following levels of leadership:

	5 PERSONHOOD		
4 PEOPLE DEVELOPMENT	RESPECT: People follow because of who you are and what you represent.	NOTE: This step is reserved for leaders who have spent years growing people and organizations. Few make it. Those who do are bigger than life.	
3 PRODUCTION	REPRODUCTION: People follow because of what you have done for them.	NOTE: This is where long-range growth occurs. Your commitment to developing leaders will insure ongoing growth to the organization and to people. Do whatever you can to achieve and stay on this level.	
2 PERMISSSION	RESULTS: People follow because of what you have done for the organization.	NOTE: This is where success is sensed by most people. They like you and what you are doing. Problems are fixed with very little effort because of momentum.	
1 POSITION	RELATIONSHIPS: People follow because they want to.	NOTE: People will follow you beyond your stated authority. This level allows work to be fun. Caution: Staying too long on this level without rising will cause highly motivated people to become restless.	
	RIGHTS: People follow because they have to.	NOTE: Your influence will not extend beyond the lines of your job description. The longer you stay here, the higher the turnover and the lower the morale.	

Level 1: Position—People Follow
Because They Have To

This is the basic entry level of leadership. The only influence you have is that which comes with a title. People who stay at this level get into territorial rights, protocol, tradition, and organizational charts. These things are not negative unless they become the basis for authority and influence, but they are poor substitutes for leadership skills.

A person may be "in control" because he has been appointed to a position. In that position he may have authority. But real leadership is more than having authority; it is more than having the technical training and following the proper procedures. Real leadership is being the person others will gladly and confidently follow. A real leader knows the difference between being the boss and being a leader.

- The boss drives his workers; the leader coaches them.
- The boss depends upon authority; the leader on goodwill.
- The boss inspires fear; the leader inspires enthusiasm.
- The boss says "I"; the leader, "we."
- The boss fixes the blame for the breakdown; the leader fixes the breakdown.

Characteristics of a "Positional Leader"

Security is based on title, not talent. The story is told of a private in World War I who shouted on the battlefield, "Put out that match!" only to find to his chagrin that the offender was General "Black Jack" Pershing. When the private, who feared severe punishment, tried to stammer out his apology, General Pershing patted him on the back and said, "That's all right, son. Just be glad I'm not a second lieutenant." The point should be clear. The higher the person's level of true ability and the resulting influence, the more secure and confident he becomes.

This level is often gained by appointment. All other levels are gained by ability. Leo Durocher was coaching at first base in an exhibition game the Giants were playing at West Point. One noisy cadet kept shouting at Leo and doing his best to upset him.

"Hey, Durocher," he hollered. "How did a little squirt like you get into the major leagues?"

Leo shouted back, "My congressman appointed me!"[2]

People will not follow a positional leader beyond his stated authority. They will only do what they have to do when they are required to do it. Low morale is always present. When the leader lacks confidence, the followers lack commitment. They are like the little boy who was asked by Billy Graham how to find the nearest post office. When the lad told him, Dr. Graham thanked him and said, "If you'll come to the convention center this evening you can hear me telling everyone how to get to heaven."

"I don't think I'll be there," the boy replied. "You don't even know your way to the post office."

Positional leaders have more difficulty working with volunteers, white collar workers, and younger people. Volunteers don't have to work in the organization so there is no monetary leverage that a positional leader can use to make them respond. White collar workers are used to participating in decision-making and resent dictatorial leadership. Baby boomers in particular are unimpressed with symbols of authority.

The following characteristics must be exhibited with excellence on this level before you can advance to the next level.

Level 1: Position/Rights

- Know your job description thoroughly.
- Be aware of the history of the organization.
- Relate the organization's history to the people of the organization (in other words, be a team player).
- Accept responsibility.
- Do your job with consistent excellence.
- Do more than expected.
- Offer creative ideas for change and improvement.

LEVEL 2: PERMISSION—PEOPLE FOLLOW
BECAUSE THEY WANT TO

Fred Smith says, "Leadership is getting people to work for you when they are not obligated."[3] That will only happen when you climb to the second level of influence. People don't care how much you know until they know how much you care. Leadership begins with the heart, not the head. It flourishes with a meaningful relationship, not more regulations.

A person on the "permission" level will lead by interrelationships. The agenda is not the pecking order but people development. On this level, the leader donates time, energy, and focus on the follower's needs and desires. A wonderful illustration of why it's so critical to put people and their needs first is found in the story of Henry Ford in Amitai Etzioni's book, *Modern Organizations*: "He made a perfect car, the Model T, that ended the need for any other car. He was totally product-oriented. He wanted to fill the world with Model T cars. But when people started coming to him and saying, 'Mr. Ford, we'd like a different color car,' he remarked, 'You can have any color you want as long as it's black.' And that's when the decline started."

People who are unable to build solid, lasting relationships will soon discover that they are unable to sustain long, effective leadership. Needless to say, you can love people without leading them, but you cannot lead people without loving them.

Caution! Don't try to skip a level. The most often skipped level is 2, *Permission*. For example, a husband goes from level 1, *Position*, a wedding day title, to level 3, *Production*. He becomes a great provider for the family, but in the process he neglects the essential relationships that hold a family together. The family disintegrates and so does the husband's business. Relationships involve a process that provides the glue and much of the staying power for long-term, consistent production.

The following characteristics must be mastered on this level before you can advance to the next one.

Level 2: Permission/Relationship
- Possess a genuine love for people.
- Make those who work with you more successful.
- See through other people's eyes.
- Love people more than procedures.
- Do "win-win" or don't do it.
- Include others in your journey.
- Deal wisely with difficult people.

LEVEL 3: PRODUCTION—PEOPLE FOLLOW BECAUSE OF WHAT YOU HAVE DONE FOR THE ORGANIZATION

On this level things begin to happen, good things. Profit

increases. Morale is high. Turnover is low. Needs are being met. Goals are being realized. Accompanying the growth is the "big mo"—momentum. Leading and influencing others is fun. Problems are solved with minimum effort. Fresh statistics are shared on a regular basis with the people who undergird the growth of the organization. Everyone is results-oriented. In fact, results are the main reason for the activity.

This is a major difference between levels 2 and 3. On the "relationship" level, people get together just to get together. There is no other objective. On the "results" level, people come together to accomplish a purpose. They like to get together to get together, but they love to get together to accomplish something. In other words, they are results-oriented.

The following characteristics must be mastered with excellence before you can advance to the next level.

Level 3: Production/Results

- Initiate and accept responsibility for growth.
- Develop and follow a statement of purpose.
- Make your job description and energy an integral part of the statement of purpose.
- Develop accountability for results, beginning with yourself.
- Know and do the things that give a high return.

- Communicate the strategy and vision of the organization.
- Become a change-agent and understand timing.
- Make the difficult decisions that will make a difference.

LEVEL 4: PEOPLE DEVELOPMENT—PEOPLE FOLLOW BECAUSE OF WHAT YOU HAVE DONE FOR THEM

A leader is great, not because of his or her power, but because of his or her ability to empower others. Success without a successor is failure. A worker's main responsibility is doing the work himself. A leader's responsibility is developing others to do the work. The true leader can be recognized because somehow his people consistently demonstrate superior performances.

Loyalty to the leader reaches its highest peak when the follower has personally grown through the mentorship of the leader. Note the progression: At level 2, the follower loves the leader; at level 3, the follower admires the leader; at level 4, the follower is loyal to the leader. Why? You win people's hearts by helping them grow personally.

The core of leaders who surround you should all be people you have personally touched or helped to develop in some way. When that happens, love and loyalty will be exhibited by those closest to you and by those who are touched by your key leaders.

There is, however, a potential problem of moving up the levels of influence as a leader and becoming comfortable with the group of people you have developed around you. Many new people may view you as a "position" leader because you have had no contact with them. These two suggestions will help you become a people developer:

1. *Walk slowly through the crowd.* Have some way of keeping in touch with everyone.

2. *Develop key leaders.* I systematically meet with and teach those who are influencers within the organization. They in turn pass on to others what I have given them.

The characteristics that must be mastered at this level are listed below.

Level 4: People Development/Reproduction

- Realize that people are your most valuable asset.
- Place a priority on developing people.
- Be a model for others to follow.
- Pour your leadership efforts into the top 20 percent of your people.
- Expose key leaders to growth opportunities.
- Attract other winners/producers to the common goal.
- Surround yourself with an inner core that complements your leadership.

Level 5: Personhood—People Follow Because of Who You Are and What You Represent

Most of us have not yet arrived at this level. Only a lifetime of proven leadership will allow us to sit at level 5 and reap the rewards that are eternally satisfying. I do know this—some day I want to sit atop this level. It's achievable.

The following characteristics define the Level 5 leader.

Level 5: Personhood/Respect

- Your followers are loyal and sacrificial.
- You have spent years mentoring and molding leaders.
- You have become a statesman/consultant, and are sought out by others.
- Your greatest joy comes from watching others grow and develop.
- You transcend the organization.

Climbing the Steps of Leadership

Here are some additional insights on the leadership-levels process:

The higher you go, the longer it takes.

Each time there is a change in your job or you join a new circle of friends, you start on the lowest level and begin to work yourself up the steps.

THE HIGHER YOU GO, THE HIGHER THE LEVEL OF COMMITMENT.

This increase in commitment is a two-way street. Greater commitment is demanded not only from you, but from the other individuals involved. When either the leader or the follower is unwilling to make the sacrifices a new level demands, influence will begin to decrease.

THE HIGHER YOU GO, THE EASIER IT IS TO LEAD.

Notice the progression from level two through level four. The focus goes from liking you to liking what you do for the common interest of all concerned (to liking what you do for them personally). Each level climbed by the leader and the followers adds another reason why people will want to follow.

THE HIGHER YOU GO, THE GREATER THE GROWTH.

Growth can only occur when effective change takes place. Change will become easier as you climb the levels of leadership. As you rise, other people will allow and even assist you in making the needed changes.

YOU NEVER LEAVE THE BASE LEVEL.

Each level stands upon the previous one and will crumble if the lower level is neglected. For example, if you move from a permission (relationships) level to a production (results) level and stop caring for the people who are following you and helping you produce, they might begin to develop a feeling of being used. As you move up in the levels, the deeper and more solid your leadership will be with a person or group of people.

IF YOU ARE LEADING A GROUP OF PEOPLE, YOU WILL
NOT BE ON THE SAME LEVEL WITH EVERYONE.

Not every person will respond the same way to your leadership.

FOR YOUR LEADERSHIP TO REMAIN EFFECTIVE, IT IS
ESSENTIAL THAT YOU TAKE THE OTHER INFLUENCERS
WITHIN THE GROUP WITH YOU TO THE HIGHER LEVELS.

The collective influence of you and the other leaders will bring the rest along. If this does not happen, divided interest and loyalty will occur within the group.

YOU MUST KNOW WHAT LEVEL YOU ARE ON
AT THIS MOMENT.

Since you will be on different levels with different people, you need to know which people are on which level. If the biggest influencers within the organization are on the highest levels and are supportive of you, then your success in leading others will be attainable. If the best influencers are on the highest levels and not supportive, then problems will soon arise.

Everyone is a leader because everyone influences someone. Not everyone will become a great leader, but everyone can become a better leader. Are you willing to unleash your leadership potential? Will you use your leadership skills to better mankind?

My Influence

My life shall touch a dozen lives
Before this day is done.
Leave countless marks of good or ill,
E'er sets the evening sun.

This, the wish I always wish,
The prayer I always pray:
Lord, may my life help other lives
It touches by the way.[4]

9

HOW CAN I EXTEND MY INFLUENCE?

The act of empowering others changes lives.

An English artist named William Wolcott went to New York in 1924 to record his impressions of that fascinating city. One morning he was visiting in the office of a former colleague when the urge to sketch came over him. Seeing some paper on his friend's desk, he asked, "May I have that?"

His friend answered, "That's not sketching paper. That's ordinary wrapping paper."

Not wanting to lose that spark of inspiration, Wolcott took the wrapping paper and said, "Nothing is ordinary if you know how to use it." On that ordinary paper Wolcott made two sketches. Later that same year, one of those same sketches sold for $500 and the other for $1,000, quite a sum for 1924.

People under the influence of an empowering person are like paper in the hands of a talented artist. No matter what they're made of, they can become treasures.

The ability to empower others is one of the keys to personal and professional success. John Craig remarked, "No matter how much work you can do, no matter how engaging your personality may be, you will not advance far in business if you cannot work through others." And business executive J. Paul Getty asserted, "It doesn't make much difference how much other knowledge or experience an executive possesses; if he is unable to achieve results through people, he is worthless as an executive."

PEOPLE UNDER THE INFLUENCE OF AN
EMPOWERING PERSON ARE LIKE PAPER IN THE HANDS
OF A TALENTED ARTIST.

When you become an empowerer, you work with and through people, but you do much more. You enable others to reach the highest levels in their personal and professional development. Simply defined, empowering is giving your influence to others for the purpose of personal and organizational growth. It's sharing yourself—your influence, position, power, and opportunities—with others for the purpose of investing in their lives so that they can function at their best. It's seeing people's potential, sharing your resources with them, and showing them that you believe in them completely.

You may already be empowering some people in your

life without knowing it. When you entrust your spouse with an important decision and then cheerfully back him up, that's empowering. When you decide that your child is ready to cross the street by herself and give her your permission to do so, you have empowered her. When you delegate a challenging job to an employee and give her the authority she needs to get it done, you have empowered her.

The act of empowering others changes lives, and it's a win-win situation for you and the people you empower. Giving others your authority isn't like giving away an object, such as your car, for example. If you give away your car, you're stuck. You no longer have transportation. But empowering others by giving them your authority has the same effect as sharing information: You haven't lost anything. You have increased the ability of others without decreasing yourself.

QUALIFICATIONS OF AN EMPOWERER

Just about everyone has the potential to become an empowerer, but you cannot empower everyone. The process works only when certain conditions are met. You must have:

POSITION

You cannot empower people whom you don't lead. Leadership expert Fred Smith explained, "Who can give permission for another person to succeed? A person in authority. Others can encourage, but permission comes only from an authority figure: a parent, boss, or pastor."

RELATIONSHIP

It has been said that relationships are forged, not formed. They require time and common experience. If you have made the effort to connect with people, then by the time you're ready to empower them, your relationship should be solid enough for you to be able to lead them. And as you do, remember what Ralph Waldo Emerson wrote, "Every man [or woman] is entitled to be valued by his [or her] best moments." When you value people and your relationships with them, you lay the foundation for empowering others.

RESPECT

Relationships cause people to want to be with you, but respect causes them to want to be empowered by you. Mutual respect is essential to the empowerment process. Psychiatrist Ari Kiev summed it up this way: "Everyone wants to feel that he counts for something and is important to someone. Invariably, people will give their love, respect, and attention to the person who fills that need." When you believe in people, care about them, and trust them, they know it. And that respect inspires them to want to follow where you lead.

Commitment

The last quality a leader needs to become an empowerer is commitment. US Air executive Ed McElroy stressed that "commitment gives us new power. No matter what comes to us—sickness, poverty, or disaster, we never turn our eye from the goal." The process of empowering others isn't always easy, especially when you start doing it for the first time. It's a road that has many bumps and sidetracks. But it is one that's worth traveling because the rewards are so great. Remember: when you empower people, you're not influencing just them; you're influencing all the people they influence. That's impact!

The Right Attitude

One more crucial element of empowering needs to be in place if you want to become a successful leader: You need to have the right attitude.

Many people neglect to empower others because they are insecure. They are afraid of losing their jobs to the people they mentor. They don't want to be replaced or displaced, even if it means that they would be able to move up to a higher position and leave their current one to be filled by the person they mentor. They're afraid of change. But change is part of empowerment—for the people you empower and for yourself. If you want to go up, there are things you have to be willing to give up.

WHEN IT COMES DOWN TO IT, EMPOWERING LEADERSHIP IS SOMETIMES THE ONLY REAL ADVANTAGE ONE ORGANIZATION HAS OVER ANOTHER IN OUR COMPETITIVE SOCIETY.

If you're not sure about where you stand in terms of your attitude toward the changes involved with empowering others, answer these questions:

QUESTIONS TO ASK BEFORE YOU GET STARTED

1. Do I believe in people and feel that they are my organization's most appreciable asset?
2. Do I believe that empowering others can accomplish more than individual achievement?
3. Do I actively search for potential leaders to empower?
4. Would I be willing to raise others to a level higher than my own level of leadership?
5. Would I be willing to invest time developing people who have leadership potential?
6. Would I be willing to let others get credit for what I taught them?
7. Do I allow others freedom of personality and process, or do I have to be in control?

8. Would I be willing to publicly give my authority and influence to potential leaders?

9. Would I be willing to let others work me out of a job?

10. Would I be willing to hand the leadership baton to the people I empower and truly root for them?

If you answer no to more than a couple of these questions, you may need an attitude adjustment. You need to believe in others enough to give them all you can and in yourself enough to know that it won't hurt you. Just remember that as long as you continue to grow and develop yourself, you'll always have something to give, and you won't need to worry about being displaced.

HOW TO EMPOWER OTHERS TO THEIR POTENTIAL

Once you have confidence in yourself and in the persons you wish to empower, you're ready to start the process. Your goal should be to hand over relatively small, simple tasks in the beginning and progressively increase their responsibilities and authority. The greener the people you're working with, the more time the process will take. But no matter whether they are raw recruits or seasoned veterans, it's still important to take them through the whole process. Use the following steps to guide you as you empower others:

1. EVALUATE THEM

The place to start when empowering people is to evaluate them. If you give inexperienced people too much authority too soon, you can set them up to fail. If you move too slowly with people who have lots of experience, you can frustrate and demoralize them.

Remember that all people have the potential to succeed. Your job is to see the potential, find out what they lack to develop it, and equip them with what they need. As you evaluate the people you intend to empower, look at these areas:

Knowledge. Think about what people need to know in order to do any task you intend to give them. Don't take for granted that they know all that you know. Ask them questions. Give them history or background information. Cast a vision by giving them the big picture of how their actions fit into the organization's mission and goals. Knowledge is not only power; it's empowering.

Skill. Examine the skill level of the people you desire to empower. Nothing is more frustrating than being asked to do things for which you have no ability. Your job as the empowerer is to find out what the job requires and make sure your people have what they need to succeed.

Desire. Greek philosopher Plutarch remarked, "The richest soil, if uncultivated, produces the rankest weeds." No amount of skill, knowledge, or potential can help people succeed if they don't have the desire to be successful. But when desire is present, empowerment is easy. As seventeenth-century French essayist Jean La Fontaine wrote, "Man is made so that whenever anything fires his soul, impossibilities vanish."

2. Model for Them

Even people with knowledge, skill, and desire need to know what's expected of them, and the best way to inform them is to show them. People do what people see.

The people you desire to empower need to see what it looks like to fly. As their mentor, you have the best opportunity to show them. Model the attitude and work ethic you would like them to embrace. And anytime you can include them in your work, take them along with you. There is no better way to help them learn and understand what you want them to do.

3. Give Them Permission to Succeed

As a leader and influencer, you may believe that everyone wants to be successful and automatically strives for success, probably as you have. But not everyone you influence will think the same way you do. You have to help others believe that they can succeed and show them that you want them to succeed. How do you do that?

Expect it. Author and professional speaker Danny Cox advised, "The important thing to remember is that if you don't have that inspired enthusiasm that is contagious—whatever you do have is also contagious." People can sense your underlying attitude no matter what you say or do. If you have an expectation for your people to be successful, they will know it.

Verbalize it. People need to hear you tell them that you believe in them and want them to succeed. Tell them often that you know they are going to make it. Send them encouraging notes. Become a positive prophet of their success. And reinforce your thoughts as often as you can.

Once people recognize and understand that you genuinely want to see them succeed and are committed to helping them, they will begin to believe they can accomplish what you give them to do.

4. TRANSFER AUTHORITY TO THEM

Many people are willing to give others responsibility. They gladly delegate tasks to them. But empowering others is more than sharing your workload. It's sharing your power and ability to get things done.

Management expert Peter Drucker asserted, "No executive has ever suffered because his subordinates were strong and effective." People become strong and effective only when they are given the opportunity to make decisions, initiate actions, solve problems, and meet challenges. When it comes down to it, empowering leadership is sometimes the only real advantage one organization has over another in our competitive society.

5. Publicly Show Your Confidence in Them

When you first transfer authority to the people you empower, you need to tell them that you believe in them, and you need to do it publicly. Public recognition lets them know that you believe they will succeed. But it also lets the other people they're working with know that they have your support and that your authority backs them up. It's a tangible way of sharing (and spreading) your influence.

As you raise up leaders, show them and their followers that they have your confidence and authority. And you will find that they quickly become empowered to succeed.

6. Supply Them with Feedback

Although you need to publicly praise your people, you can't let them go very long without giving them honest, positive feedback. Meet with them privately to coach them through their mistakes, miscues, and misjudgments. At first, some people may have a difficult time. During that early period, be a grace giver. Try to give them what they need, not what they deserve. And applaud any progress that they make. People do what gets praised.

7. RELEASE THEM TO CONTINUE ON THEIR OWN

No matter who you are working to empower—your employees, children, colleagues, or spouse—your ultimate aim should be to release them to make good decisions and succeed on their own. And that means giving them as much freedom as possible as soon as they are ready for it.

President Abraham Lincoln was a master at empowering his leaders. For example, when he appointed General Ulysses S. Grant as commander of the Union armies in 1864, he sent him this message: "I neither ask nor desire to know anything of your plans. Take the responsibility and act, and call on me for assistance."

That's the attitude you need as an empowerer. Give authority and responsibility, and offer assistance as needed. The person who has been the most empowering in my life is my father, Melvin Maxwell. He always encouraged me to be the best person I could be, and he gave me his permission and his power whenever he could. Years later when we talked about it, my father told me his philosophy: "I never consciously limited you as long as I knew what you were doing was morally right." Now that's an empowering attitude!

The Results of Empowerment

If you head up any kind of organization—a business, club, church, or family—learning to empower others is one of the most important things you'll ever do as its leader. Empowerment has an incredibly high return. It not only helps the individuals you raise up by making them more confident, energetic, and productive, but it also has the ability to improve your life, give you additional freedom, and promote the growth and health of your organization.

As you empower others, you will find that most aspects of your life will change for the better. Empowering others can free you personally to have more time for the important things in your life, increase the effectiveness of your organization, increase your influence with others and, best of all, make an incredibly positive impact on the lives of the people you empower.

10

HOW CAN I MAKE MY
LEADERSHIP LAST?

A leader's lasting value is measured by succession.

I n 1997, one of the finest business leaders in the world
died. His name was Roberto Goizueta, and he was the
chairman and chief executive of the Coca-Cola Company.
In a speech he gave to the Executives' Club of Chicago a
few months before he died, Goizueta made this statement:
"A billion hours ago, human life appeared on Earth. A billion minutes ago, Christianity emerged. A billion seconds
ago, the Beatles performed on 'The Ed Sullivan Show.' A
billion Coca-Colas ago . . . was yesterday morning. And the
question we are asking ourselves now is, 'What must we do
to make a billion Coca-Colas ago this morning?'"

Making Coca-Cola the best company in the world was
Goizueta's lifelong quest, one he was still pursuing dili-
gently when he suddenly, unexpectedly died. Companies
that lose a CEO often go into turmoil, especially if his

departure is unexpected, as Goizueta's was. Shortly before his death, Goizueta said in an interview with the *Atlanta Journal-Constitution* that retirement was "not on my radar screen. As long as I'm having the fun I'm having, as long as I have the energy necessary, as long as I'm not keeping people from their day in the sun, and as long as the board wants me to stay on, I will stay on." Just months after the interview, he was diagnosed with cancer. Six weeks later, he died.

Upon Goizueta's death, former president Jimmy Carter observed, "Perhaps no other corporate leader in modern times has so beautifully exemplified the American dream. He believed that in America, all things are possible. He lived that dream. And because of his extraordinary leadership skills, he helped thousands of others realize their dreams as well."

GOIZUETA'S LEGACY

The legacy left to the company by Goizueta is incredible. When he took over Coca-Cola in 1981, the company's value was $4 billion. Under Goizueta's leadership, it rose to $150 billion. That's an increase in value of more than 3,500 percent! Coca-Cola became the second most valuable corporation in America, ahead of the car makers, the oil companies, Microsoft, Wal-Mart, and all the rest. The only company more valuable was General Electric. Many of Coke's stockholders became millionaires many times over. Emory University in Atlanta, whose portfolio contains a large block of Coca-Cola stock, now has an endowment comparable to that of Harvard.

But high stock value wasn't the most significant thing Goizueta gave to the Coca-Cola company. Instead it was the way he left a legacy. When the CEO's death was announced, there was no panic among Coca-Cola stockholders. Paine Webber analyst Emanuel Goldman said that Goizueta "prepared the company for his not being there as well as any executive I've ever seen."

How did he do it? First, by making the company as strong as he possibly could. Second, by preparing a successor for the top position named Douglas Ivester. Mickey H. Gramig, writer for the *Atlanta Constitution,* reported, "Unlike some companies, which face a crisis when the top executive leaves or dies, Coca-Cola is expected to retain its status as one of the world's most admired corporations. Goizueta had groomed Ivester to follow his footsteps since the Georgia native's 1994 appointment to the company's No. 2 post. And as an indication of how strongly Wall Street felt about Coca-Cola's footings, the company's stock barely rippled six weeks ago when Goizueta was diagnosed with lung cancer."[1]

Doug Ivester, an accountant by training, started his career with Coca-Cola in 1979 as the assistant controller. Four years later, he was named chief financial officer. He was known for his exceptional financial creativity, and he was a major force in Goizueta's ability to revolutionize the company's approach to investment and the handling of debt. By 1989, Goizueta must have decided that Ivester had untapped potential, because he moved him out of his strictly financial role and sent him to Europe to obtain operating and international experience. A year later, Goizueta brought him back and named him president of Coca-Cola USA, where he oversaw expenditures and marketing. From there he continued to groom Ivester, and in 1994, there could be no doubt that Ivester would follow Goizueta into the top position. Goizueta made him president and chief operating officer.

What Roberto Goizueta did was very unusual. Few chief executives of companies today develop strong leaders and groom them to take over the organization. John S. Wood, a consultant at Egon Zehnder International Inc., has noted that "companies have not in the recent past been investing as heavily in bringing people up. If they're not able to grow them, they have to go get them." So why was Roberto Goizueta different? He knew the positive effect of mentoring firsthand.

Roberto Goizueta was born in Cuba and educated at Yale, where he earned a degree in chemical engineering. When he returned to Havana in 1954, he answered a newspaper ad for a bilingual chemist. The company hiring turned out to be Coca-Cola. By 1966, he had become vice president of technical research and development at the company's headquarters in Atlanta. He was the youngest man ever to hold such a position in the company. But in the early 1970s, something even more important happened. Robert W. Woodruff, the patriarch of Coca-Cola, took Goizueta under his wing and began developing him. In 1975, Goizueta became the executive vice president of the company's technical division and took on other corporate responsibilities, such as overseeing legal affairs. And in 1980, with Woodruff's blessing, Goizueta became president and chief operating officer. One year later he was the chairman and chief executive. The reason Goizueta so confidently selected, developed, and groomed a successor in the 1990s is that he was building on the legacy that he had received in the 1970s.

LEADERS WHO LEAVE A LEGACY OF SUCCESSION . . .

Leaders who leave a legacy of succession for their organization do the following:

LEAD THE ORGANIZATION WITH A "LONG VIEW"

Just about anybody can make an organization look good for a moment—by launching a flashy new program or product, drawing crowds to a big event, or slashing the budget to boost the bottom line. But leaders who leave a legacy take a different approach. They lead with tomorrow as well as today in mind. That's what Goizueta did. He planned to keep leading as long as he was effective, yet he prepared his successor anyway. He always looked out for the best interests of the organization and its stockholders.

CREATE A LEADERSHIP CULTURE

The most stable companies have strong leaders at every level of the organization. The only way to develop such widespread leadership is to make developing leaders a part of your culture. That is a strong part of Coca-Cola's legacy. How many other successful companies do you know about that have had a succession of leaders come up within the ranks of their own organization?

PAY THE PRICE TODAY TO ASSURE SUCCESS TOMORROW

There is no success without sacrifice. Each organization is unique, and that dictates what the price will be. But any leader who wants to help his organization must be willing to pay that price to ensure lasting success.

VALUE TEAM LEADERSHIP ABOVE
INDIVIDUAL LEADERSHIP

No matter how good he is, no leader can do it all alone. Just as in sports a coach needs a team of good players to win, an organization needs a team of good *leaders* to succeed. The larger the organization, the stronger, larger, and deeper the team of leaders needs to be.

WALK AWAY FROM THE ORGANIZATION
WITH INTEGRITY

In the case of Coca-Cola, the leader didn't get the opportunity to walk away because he died an untimely death. But if he had lived, I believe Goizueta would have done just that. When it's a leader's time to leave the organization, he has got to be willing to walk away and let his successor do his own thing. Meddling only hurts him and the organization.

FEW LEADERS PASS IT ON

Max Dupree, author of *Leadership Is an Art,* declared, "Succession is one of the key responsibilities of leadership." Yet of all the characteristics of leadership, legacy is the one that the fewest leaders seem to learn. Achievement comes to someone when he is able to do great things for himself. Success comes when he empowers followers to do great things *with* him. Significance comes when he develops leaders to do great things *for* him. But a legacy is created only when a person puts his organization into the position to do great things *without* him.

I learned the importance of legacy the hard way. Because the church grew so much while I was in my first leadership position in Hillham, Indiana, I thought I was a success. When I began there, we had only three people in attendance. For three years, I built up that church, reached out to the community, and influenced many people's lives. When I left, our average attendance was in the high two hundreds, and our record was more than three hundred people. I had programs in place, and everything looked rosy to me. I thought I had really done something significant.

Eighteen months after I had moved to my second church, I had lunch with a friend I hadn't seen in a while, and he had just spent some time in Hillham. I asked him about how things were going back there, and I was surprised to hear his answer.

"Not too good," he answered.

"Really?" I said. "Why? Things were going great when I left. What's wrong?"

"Well," he said, "it's kind of fallen off. Some of the programs you got started kind of petered out. The church is running only about a hundred people. It might get even smaller before it's all over."

That really bothered me. A leader hates to see something that he put his sweat, blood, and tears into starting to fail. At first, I got ticked off at the leader who followed me. But then it hit me. If I had done a really good job there, it wouldn't matter what kind of leader followed me, good or bad. The fault was really mine. I hadn't set up the organization to succeed after I left. It was the first time I realized the significance of legacy.

PARADIGM SHIFT

After that, I started to look at leadership in a whole new way. Every leader eventually leaves his organization—one way or another. He may change jobs, get promoted, or retire. And even if a person refuses to retire, he is going to die. That made me realize that part of my job as a leader was to start preparing my people and organization for what inevitably lies ahead. That prompted me to change my focus from leading followers to developing leaders. My lasting value, like that of any leader, would be measured by my ability to give the organization a smooth succession.

My best personal succession story concerns my departure from Skyline Church. When I first arrived there in 1981, I made one of my primary goals the identification and development of leaders because I knew that our success depended on it. Over the fourteen years I was there, my staff and I developed literally hundreds of outstanding leaders, both volunteers and staff.

One of my greatest joys in life is knowing that Skyline is stronger now than when I left in 1995. Jim Garlow, who succeeded me as the senior pastor, is doing a wonderful job there. In the fall of 1997, Jim asked me to come back to Skyline and speak at a fund-raising banquet for the next phase of the building project, and I was delighted to honor his request.

About 4,100 people attended the event at the San Diego Convention Center, located on the city's beautiful bay. My wife, Margaret, and I really enjoyed the chance to see and talk with so many of our old friends. And of course, I felt privileged to be the evening's keynote speaker. It was quite a celebration—and quite a success. People pledged more than $7.8 million toward the building of the church's new facility.

As soon as I finished speaking, Margaret and I slipped out of the ballroom. We wanted the night to belong to Jim, since he was now the leader of Skyline. Because of that, we knew it would be best if we made a quick exit before the program was over. Descending the stairs, I grabbed her hand and gave it a squeeze. It was wonderful to know that what we started all those years ago was still going on. It's like my friend Chris Musgrove says, "Success is not measured by what you're leaving to, but by what you are leaving behind."

When all is said and done, your ability as a leader will not be judged by what you achieved personally or even by what your team accomplished during your tenure. You will be judged by how well your people and your organization did after you were gone. Your lasting value will be measured by succession.

NOTES

Chapter 1
1. John F. Love, *McDonald's: Behind the Arches* (New York: Bantam Books, 1986).

Chapter 2
1. "The Champ," *Reader's Digest*, January 1972, 109.

Chapter 4
1. R. Earl Allen, *Let It Begin in Me* (Nashville: Broadman Press, 1985).

Chapter 5
1. E. M. Swift, "Odd Man Out," *Sports Illustrated*, 92–96.
2. Robert Shaw, "Tough Trust," *Leader to Leader* (Winter 1997), 46–54.

Chapter 7
1. Quoted at www.abcnews.com on 4 February 1998.
2. Thomas A. Stewart, "Brain Power: Who Owns It . . . How They Profit from It," *Fortune*, 17 March 1997, 105–6.

Chapter 8
1. Robert Dilenschneider, *Power and Influence: Mastering the Art of Persuasion* (New York: Prentice Hall, 1990).
2. E. C. McKenzie, *Quips and Quotes* (Grand Rapids: Baker, 1980).
3. Fred Smith, *Learning to Lead* (Waco: Word, 1986), 117.
4. John C. Maxwell, *Be a People Person* (Wheaton: Victor, 1989).

Chapter 10
1. Mickey H. Gramig, *Atlanta Constitution*, 10 November 1997.

About the Author

John C. Maxwell, an internationally regarded expert on leadership, speaks to hundreds of thousands of people on six continents each year. He has communicated his leadership principles to Fortune 500 companies, heads of state, and the United States Military Academy at West Point, as well as to university and professional sports organizations.

Dr. Maxwell is the founder of Injoy Stewardship Services and EQUIP, a non-profit organization that teaches leadership worldwide. He is also a *New York Times* and *Business Week* best-selling author of more than thirty books with over nine million copies sold. Two of his books, *Developing the Leader Within You* and *The 21 Irrefutable Laws of Leadership*, are million sellers.